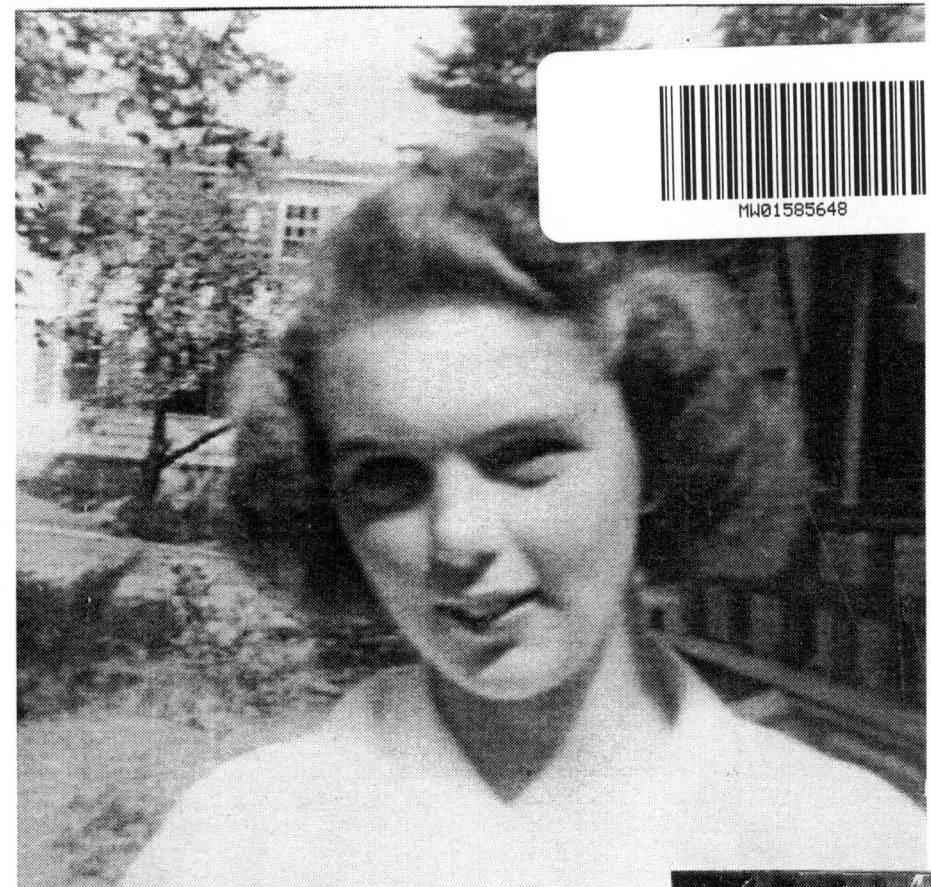

Vera Payson
Summer of 1942

Left: Four Generations
Great-grandmother Sarah Ricker,
Grandmother Ella Mathieson,
Son John and Father Louis M.

Right:
Robert Case and Louis M.,
*summer of 1942 at
Old Orchard Beach, Maine*

One Sunday Morning

by Louis R. Mathieson

*Dedicated to Vera (Payson) Mathieson,
the love of my life*

It hasn't been easy for Vera. I was a rough character, and it has taken a life time to tame. With the nightmares and hidden fears. She has been a strong Christian influence for me. She understands people, and she is constantly telling me names and the background of the people around me. One thing I have really enjoyed is her high school graduating class. Which I have attended every class reunion. I have found that our circle of friends has been this class of 1942.

REVIEWS

ONE SUNDAY MORNING began as a memoir written for Louis Mathieson's family. Its title derives from the Sunday morning attack on Pearl Harbor where Louis was serving aboard the USS Oklahoma. When the manuscript was in its initial stage. Louie asked me to read it and to offer suggestions. It was my opinion, and that of others whom I asked to review the manuscript, that Louie's story should be told in his own words and in his own style. The format of reminiscence and the conversational tone, which so engages the reader, we felt should not be compromised by editorial intervention.

We have an opportunity, through Louie, to experience what it meant to be a member of what Tom Brokaw describes as the Greatest Generation. Louie's life journey takes us through his childhood years during the Depression, his participation as a young adult in the Civilian Conservation Corps designed by FDR to provide employment for the nation's young men, the abrupt entry of the US into World War II at Pearl Harbor, and the establishment of a peacetime world and return to home and family.

There was another Sunday morning milestone when he met Vera Payson. It is a tribute to Louie's romantic nature and good judgment of people that he recognized how important Vera would be to the rest of his life. After more than fifty years of marriage, they still represent what today's generation describes as "soul mates."

In Robert Kennedy's words, Louie dreamed of things that never were and said "why not?" Louie dreamed of "the house on the hill overlooking the water" and it came true. He dreamed of raising a fine family, and it came true. ONE SUNDAY MORNING reveals not only the details of that "day of infamy," but also the indomitable spirit and accomplishment of one of its survivors.

Eloise J. Law, PhD.
Professor Emeritus, State University of New York

===========================

6;30 Monday Morning
May 28, 2001

Dear Lou & Vera,

We're out at our beloved camp. I've been up long enough to get a nice fire going in the kitchen wood stove so it's up to 64 degrees here already, not that it was that cold anyway. The loons have called half-heartedly, a couple of times since I awoke The fog is masking the lake.

Last night I finished reading every page of your book. Lou thank you, thank you, thank you for writing it, and for handing us a copy. How appropriate that I have just finished reliving your life, so far, on Memorial Day! My reaction to your story is profound and deep. I've deep-seated respect for you almost since we first met. (1989 or 1990), but the depth of my respect for now has gone to infinity.

Oh, I recognized bits and pieces of what you had, over time, shared with us/me already, but the full impact set in early on in reading your book. You certainly are a "survivor" in the deepest sense of the word! And best of all, through it all, you have always given your all to such a wide spectrum, to your community and to your church.

I so hope that you will somehow come to terms with your "right now" distress over your local church situation; view it as just another small blip on the screen of life and be able to attend some church, in peace and surrounded by Christ's unlimited love that he has for you, Lou.

To write more would only dilute the true feelings I have so, may the Lord's Peace be with you, Lou & Vera.

Love

H.T. Griffen
P. O. Box 901
Union, Maine 04862-0901
Herb & Audrey Griffen

August 20, 2000

Dear Louie and Vera,

Just finished talking to you on the phone, and I want to get this check off to you pronto.

We enjoyed your book so much. It was just like listening to you say it. The content was great. The part of you traveling across country after Pearl Harbor with nothing to eat for days, no decent clothing, just really tore at me.

How Bob would have enjoyed your book! I am so glad we've remained friends; you must know Bubber thinks the world of you. I've been truly blessed, and after reading your book, I know you have been

Mrs. Robert R. Kinderman
4680 Island View Dr.
Oshkosh, Wisconsin, 54901
Love you both Peg

= =

September 20, 2001

Hi Louie and Vera,

I wanted to thank you for the copy of your book. I admire your memory for the names and places, and your very descriptive information regarding all those engines and complicated machinery and pumps you so ably kept in operation which was so necessary for us to win that war.

It's obvious you have a great talent as a mechanic and engineer, and with today's economy, you could be wealthy performing those job in all types of industry.

I certainly can relate to your difficult childhood during the Depression while growing up in the twenties and thirties. We also had a tough time managing, as my father was sickly with a bad heart condition. He was always able to maintain a job, and there was plenty to eat and hand-me-down clothes from my mother's family. Your experience was much more traumatic with your father's absence and your mother the sole support.

I hope the young people in your family, as well as other people reading this account, can visualize what you endured and how you left school to enter the CCC (Civilian Conservation Corp), which relieved your mother and put a meal on the table after a hard day's work, under very difficult weather conditions living in very inadequate living quarters.

You accepted these unusual tasks and always look forward to a better life with determination and trust in God.

Your next venture to join the US Navy was so exciting, and filled with horrors of Pearl Harbor, and your survival from the sinking ship.

By that time in your young life, you must have wondered what next can happen! It's a major disaster, it's frightening and I am damn lucky to still be alive.

I also relate to your landing in Noumea, New Caladonia, as that is where we landed for staging before shipping out to Guadalcanal shortly after the island was secured by the Marines and infantry. I was in the 13th Fighter Command, we started our operations there, than on to many stops in New Guinea, and finally winding up in the Philippines.

We had P38 fighters and B25 bombers as part of the 13th, and we were high-speed radio operators in headquarters.

I was most interested in your explanation of the diesel engines and pumps as I am quite mechanical and ran a service shop with my business selling power equipment.

I was most interested with your many jobs in Rockland, and life as a family man! You studied hard to get your diploma from high school, and took so many courses to accomplish your trade and licenses you acquired.

You were most fortunate to meet such a fine lady and wife. I am sure she supported all those trying years raising a family, building your house and making a success of your life, and a loving family.

You've earned your retirement go fishing and camping; best of all, give Vera a big hug for us, as we enjoy your friendship.

144 Franklin St. Lakeport, N.H. 03248
Love Bill and Eleanor

Dear Louie,

I returned your book to Betty while I was still in Rhode Island, so that she can get it back to you.

Thank you so very much for the opportunity of reading a most interesting and fascinating account of your life as a young man.

You write beautifully. I found your memories of your boyhood days and your time with the CCC (Civilian Conservation Corp) heart-rending & sensitive, as well as your experience in the war.

It was good seeing you while I was in Maine. Stay well, have a pleasant fall season & do give my very best to Vera.

Always,
Mary Lou
10 Brier Hollow, #12
Houston, Texas 770274

= =

(This Lady bought five books and sent a check for $100 with this explanation.)

Dear Louis and Vera;

The first book goes to my mom. She is 85 years and lives in Bath, ME.

I told her about it and she asked me to leave it with her. But I hadn't finished it, so I am now giving her her own copy. It sparked a conversation about her family in the depression, Which she had never told me about.

Bob felt humbled by your story—and awed and inspired.

Love Susan

(Then she writes another letter):

This is just to let you know who else I have been giving your wonderful books to.

Donald

Donald is 75 or 76. He grew up on a farm in Oregon and went into the Navy at 17/18. When he got out he used a G.I. loan to build a little house. He served in the Pacific; I don't remember the details. I met him and his wife, Madeline, and their three children. I was 22. I went to live with them for a year, while I started architecture school in Berkley, CA. Donald always had bad feelings about the Japanese after the war. Donald's family is from Sweden. He and Madeline are my dearest friends.

Bob

Bob lives in Camden. He worked with us for years at Outward Bound. Bob always says he is a fine leader. Bob believes he missed something by not serving in the military. He had three brothers and his mother is very religious; we always talk about spiritual and religious matters. We used to run about the same speed, running at Outward Bound. He was a football player at U. M. and then slimmed down to do a triathalon in Hawaii. He runs an international leadership in?????, which my Bob says is folding because of Sept 11 and no one is paying for training any more. Bob is about 50 years old.

Philip

He's about in the late 40s, He and my sister owned a dairy farm in Vermont. They did everything on that farm. They sold it when they learned the government was pouring milk down the drain. Philip is an educator, a builder and a conservationist. He helped me build a house in Cushing, ME. I met him when he was going to a contra dance in Vermont with my sister and I went too. Bob always said he was from another century, how he could use his hands.

Love Susan & Bob

= =

(I found this note on my windshield wipers)

I saw your license plate and want to thank you for your service to this great country.

I was born 6 months before Pearl Harbor and I have a lot of respect and admiration for those who gave so much to make this world what it is today

Have a great Day!

ACKNOWLEDGMENT

This account on my experiences of my life are from memory only, I don't have much to rely on as to authenticate reality. I have been mostly a do it your selfer., and not much of a letter writer. Most of my friends have died now, and although I would love to be able to contact what's left of my friends I don't have there addresses. My life after the Pearl Harbor attack was completely started new. I never returned to Minneapolis, Minn. after the war. Instead I went to Maine where I made my life. I lost my childhood friends as I didn't write to them. I am sorry to say I was a poor letter writer. The only time I ever wrote to any degree, was when I wrote to my girlfriend whom I married 56 years ago.

I want to dedicate this book to my friends of many years ago, most of them are gone now. The first one, Robert R. Kinderman, we became friends when we were Oklahoma sailors and lasted until this past February 1999, I used to call him when I was depressed, when I heard his voice it seemed to relieve my stress. We made periodic visits over to Oshkosh, Wisconsin, or over here to my house, we were like brothers. I felt like I could say any thing to him, just as I would to my brothers Harry and Everett. Next I would like to remember Mike Galdjick, brothers Malcom, Leroy, and Randolph Barber. These were my friends on board the USS Oklahoma, They lost there lives on Dec. 7, 1941. Paul Gloor was also an Oklahoma sailor, he helped me when I went to Old Orchard beach to meet my girl friend and later wife. A. G. Slagter MM 1/c He went on USS Chester, and later my brother Harry met him in San Francisco two years later and the story about how he had opened my escape hatch. He was on a submarine at that time. Then I had some friends in the CCC camp, which I would like to remember, they are Pete Peterson, from International falls, Ray Lukenbill from Northome, Minnesota, Ray was also on the USS West Virginia on Dec. 7 1941. I don't know if he survived the attack. Then there was William Orvile, August, Plate, who was on the cruiser USS Boise, A month or so before the attack. Bill was on the USS Solace a hospital ship, for treatment. The USS Boise had left Pearl Harbor for the Philippine Islands, and he was hitch hiking by air plane at the time, and was captured on Wake Island. Wake Island fell to the Japanese on Dec. 23, 1942. We had crossed the international Date line on the 18th of Dec. and the next day was Dec. 20 1941. I know because I was 20 years old on Dec. 19 1941, and I expected a birthday cake on my birthday. We were going to attack at 12 o'clock midnight. Just a few minutes before midnight admiral Nimitz recalled all units back to Pearl Harbor.

Copyright Louis R. Mathieson, 2000

INTRODUCTION

To the reader who enters my life, by reading these words. I wrote this story for my children. I want them to know how I lived my life. This is how I remember it. I have tried to put down the facts as true to the best of my knowledge. I wished so many times, that I had asked my mother about her life, before she died. I like to think that I received GOD'S blessing when I was born. It seems that what ever my dreams were about as a kid, I had the experience of living them. I always felt that I was special. As an example, when I was around thirteen years old, I was reading books by James Oliver Curwood. He wrote about the early woodsman that logged the forests of Michigan. He wrote about the virgin pine forests, and I wanted to see a virgin pine forest. As you read about my C.C.C. Camp days, you will experience the hardship that goes with the experience. My life was filled with hardship, but really I think there are other people out there that had it a lot tougher than I ever did. I feel that my life was a great romance, perhaps because I loved every minute of it. I was always an early riser, I was always afraid I would miss something, and the best part of the day was in the morning. When life was the toughest in the C.C.C. Camp, I would tell myself, that these were the best days of my life, enjoy them. I felt good, I was healthy, and I had unlimited energy.

My mother saw to it, that we had a close connection with our church. The Central Lutheran Church of Minneapolis. I was confirmed when I was around fourteen years old. I carried this bit of philosophy, it goes like this. There are three things that reach beyond the edge of the earth, The lightness of day, the darkness of night, and the long arm of GOD. I believed that if I was to do something wrong it would be at night. The U.S. Navy made us return to the ship before midnight. I made my children return home before midnight all during their high school years. Vera and I have kept a close relationship with our church the Rockland Congregational Church, during our married life. My greatest disappointment, is with the U.S. Government, when they removed prayer from our public schools. I often think how disappointed those service men, that died in battle, would feel, if they had known that this would happen. I think of all the children today that don't get any of the teachings of JESUS CHRIST OUR LORD AND SAVIOR. I recognize that, what I am writing about might not agree with other peoples experiences. What my brother wrote about in his story was some what different than mine. There is so much more to write about, than what I've put down here, maybe at a later time I might add some more. This is what I remember.

Louis R. Mathieson

©2000 Louis R. Mathieson, 4 Everett Ave., Owls Head, ME 04854 mark@bullioncoin.com

One Sunday Morning

by Louis R. Mathieson

Friday Dec. 5, 1941.

When we entered port this time, instead of tying up, where we were used to tying up, (The place where the USS Arizona tied up that day). We were placed just out board of the USS Maryland. We were at the head of the line. I was really concerned, I thought we were being set up for something The scuttle butte (information), being circulated around. We were going to have some movie people come aboard Sunday, and take some pictures of us. I was still uneasy, we were sticking out there like a sore thumb I thought it was funny, there were no aircraft carriers in port. That wasn't really too much to be concerned about as we had come in before and the carriers had gone some where else.

It was Friday and I had the liberty, and I was anxious to get shore Liberty. To pick up my picture album at May's, Red Front Cafe. As I had left it there the week before. I had been telling this Japanese girl about my C.C.C. camp experiences all summer and fall. I was really home sick for the northern forests. I had left it there because when I left her last week it was too late to take it to the Army and Navy YMCA where I could get wrapping paper to send it back home. Saturday I had the duty. My watches were from 4/00 PM TO 8 PM Saturday and from 4/00 AM to 8/00 AM Sunday morning Dec. 7 1941. I was standing my watches in the so called Ice Machines. or the refrigeration plant. To get an idea as to where that was you need to look at the ship from the port side. If you look at the tripod masts the one to the rear. At the very bottom of the ship a little forward of that, is where the Ice Machines were located. My battle station was located just under that after tripod and just below the armor deck. That was two decks below the top side, quarter deck. My relief that Sunday morning was A friend (Mike Galajdik). He had agreed to relieve me fifteen minutes early, as he knew I had this date with May, and I wanted to make that 8:00 o'clock liberty boat. May was going to show me the Royal Hawaiian Forest preserve. At this time in my life I wanted to become a Forest Ranger. I was using this opportunity to learn as much as possible about Hawaiian forestry. We had talked about this, the day before. As my locker was located in the ice machine room. I removed all of my clothes and with a towel wrapped around me and my shoes on. I went up the ladder to the main deck then across to the starboard side and then forward to the next compartment to the engineers shower room.

My brother (Harry) arrived at the same time, coming up from the evaporators, which was on the starboard side opposite the ice machines.

We were about to enter the shower stall. When the general alarm went off.

"All hands man your battle stations, "God Dam it!! Get going this is it". Just then, "Boom" the ship seemed to dip forward a little, actually the bow came up. I grabbed my shoes, and towel and ran for my battle station. Repair #5 in the machine shop. Located just over the port and starboard engine rooms.

Arriving there, my job was to close the armor hatch to the main deck, when the battle stations were fully manned. When we were hit by another torpedo. It must have hit near us, as the ship seemed to leap up about a foot and a half, or maybe just the deck under me. The noise was horrendous. There were two explosions. (I can recall seven explosions in all.) With the second hit, my feet were knocked out from under me, and I landed on deck. At this time I was really getting excited, my mind seemed to be whizzing so bad, I thought it was going to explode. I wanted to cry, but had to control it. I didn't want any body to know I was such a coward. The lights went out. They seemed to come back on again. Then another torpedo hit and they went out for good. I thought about all of that water coming in and we were going to be immersed in that filthy oil laden water with all of that sewage combined. It made me sick just to think about it. All of this was going on at once. I thought I was going to die at any moment. I tried to say the LORDS PRAYER "OUR FATHER WHO ART IN HEAVEN, HALLOWED BE THY NAME' boom boom my thoughts were scattered. I thought I'd try the TWENTY THIRD PSALM. THE LORD IS MY SHEPHERD I SHALL NOT WANT, HE LEADETH ME, BOOM BOOM, I felt like I didn't have time to say a prayer. In desperation, I said, "LORD I PLACE MY LIFE IN YOUR HANDS'. Then my mind cleared and that terrible buzzing in my head was gone. Now I could think. The officer in charge, a Mr. McCullough, Lieutenant, as I remember, wanted that armor hatch closed, as the battle stations were manned. I went up the ladder with my friend Bob Kinderman to close the hatch. We couldn't budge it, the ship had too much of a list to port, and the hatch was hinged on the port side. We called for more help, three or four us still could not close the hatch. Discouraged we returned to the machine shop.. Then one of our crew said, "This is enough for me, I am getting out of here". The officer in charge said, "Somebody stop that man". I was in his direct line of escape, I directed him into a large vertical drill press, that I was hanging on to. He hit his head and went down. I felt sorry for him, as he had done exactly what I wanted to do, but didn't have the courage too. We then had a call on our J.V. phone. The evaporators wanted two men, volunteers. They wanted help to remove the bonnets on the sea water intake valves. The evaporators were on the starboard side, and flooding the starboard side of the ship, would help to prevent the ship from capsizing. Mr. McCullough was standing right in front of me, and my friend Bob Kinderman. It was logical for him to point us out to go. My legs began to feel like rubber. I didn't want to go down there for any reason. I knew it was too late to go down there. I could see that greasy stinking pump room under the evaporators. It made me sick even in normal times. There were two first class machinist mates, who volunteered I was afraid the officer wouldn't let them go, as they were too valuable, but he did. They were very brave men. Later that day, when the ship had capsized. Sounds were heard from within the hull of the ship, tapping sounds. An effort was made to rescue these men. A burning torch was brought aboard, and they were almost through to these two men, when the cork and oil caught fire, and these two men were suffocated.

I was afraid the officer wasn't going to give the abandon ship order, and we were doomed to die right there. When the officer asked the man on the J.V. phones (Sam Smith), if he had heard anything about abandon ship. He answered in the affirmative. The officer then gave the order to abandon ship.

I was the first one up the ladder, as I had just come down from there. I tried to open that water tight door, that had been dogged down. It wouldn't open. I called for help. Five or six of us braced against the door, with our feet against the opposite wall. The door gave a little and water began to come in from all sides. I shouted, "stop we're under water".

I was born in Minneapolis, Minnesota on Dec. 19 1920 at 5;45 PM. My parents lived at 2740 34th Ave. So. My father was a boiler maker by trade, for the railroads. I believe he worked for the Soo line. His job was to crawl into those hot fire boxes in those steam engines, and plug the leaking tubes in the boilers. They were Scotch boilers. The hot gases from the fire box passed through the tubes. A leaking tube could be found by water dripping from the tubes. Because his job was so dry and sooty my father would frequent the saloons on his way home from work. He soon became alcoholic. My only recollection of him is in a drunken state. I was the third son of four boys and for some reason the apple of his eye. I could steal his whiskey and pour it down the sink, and get away with it. He would blame it on my brother Everett, or my mother. That evening when he woke up he blamed it on my brother and my mother. They had a fight and when he started to slap my mother, she ran away from him and into the bed room and when she was shutting the door to keep him away from her, she caught her fingers in the door jam, almost cutting them off. She had to go to the hospital, and when she came home their marriage was over. When I was about four years old my mother and father separated and they sold their house. I really don't know how much they received for the house. I think they got around $600.00 for it.

My mother then took her four boys on the train to Pawtucket, Rhode Island. So as to be near her mother, sisters, and brother. I can remember that train ride. We took the coach and slept on the seats. You could pull the back of one seat over so that both seats would face each other. My mother bought a very long loaf of bread and something to put on it. I can't remember what it was. We ate this for our meals, on the three or four day trip East. I remember this train was called the Midnight Flyer.

We lived in my uncles house for awhile. I think we lived on the third floor and my grand mother Ricker lived on the second floor. I remember my grandmother Sarah Ricker being very strict. She taught me how to tie my shoe laces. I did a lot of crying, and in between tears I learned. When I would be going up to our apartment, I would be very quiet when I went by her door. She would discipline me with a crack on the back side of my head. Her discipline was severe and effective. She had her good side also. I remember at Christmas time, she always sent us five dollars. Which was a lot of money in those days. One year my mother took the five dollars and bought me a pair of ice skates. I was around twelve years old. I put the skates on and went out on the ice and skated. I had watched the people skate for so long, I had learned how. I would be on the ice when the rink opened in the morning, and stayed until the rink closed 9:00 o'clock at night. In Minneapolis, every neighborhood had an ice skating rink. Some of the games we played were pump pump pull away, where one person stood in the middle, and every body would try to pass over to the other side of the rink, and not get caught by the person in the middle.

As a rule Mom tried to share grandma's money evenly with all of us. I didn't see my grandmother again until the spring of 1942. I often wondered what she thought of me. I suppose I was all right as I had asked her if she would give me her wedding ring when she died. I was some surprised when about fifteen years later I received her ring, I remember her name was engraved on the inside of the ring. Little did I know that twenty years later I would be giving it to my daughter's husband to be, to use for her wedding band. What is interesting, years later, Nancy told me, that when her house would get messy, that ring would tighten on her finger, to remind her to clean house.

We stayed in Rhode Island one year. Mom decided to move back to Minneapolis. Mom was a divorcee, and these relatives treated her as a second class citizen. That's how they looked at a divorced women in those days. It must have been pretty bad, because, when we went back to Minneapolis there wouldn't be anybody to go to for help when we needed it. It was tough. We landed back in Mpls. with no money, and no place to stay. We went to one of Mom's old friends, "the Donaldsons." Mrs. Donaldson asked her, "to get a hotel room. Mom said there were no hotel rooms available. She had to as she didn't have any money." So we stayed there. I didn't know this, but years later my brother Everett told me this story. We stayed at the Donaldson's about a week, then moved into an apartment. Mom had to get out and find a job. (As far as I know my mother never had a savings account in any bank.) Which left Harry and me to shift for our selves. I was around five and Harry was two years younger. I remember going down town and wondering around the Foshey tower which was being built at that time. There the workmen would share their lunches with us. I went to school that fall.

My mother worked in a laundry, eight to ten hours a day, on a steam press, and ironing shirts. I can remember her pay was ten dollars a week for six days work. In those days all four of us boys slept in the same bed, only cross ways, for more room. I made sure I was in the middle, so I would be warm. We didn't always have heat in the house. Our food wasn't that good either. There were a lot of times that we went to bed with out supper.. There was never any fruit. One winter we came down with the seven year itch, it could have been scurvy. The four of us would have this rash all over our body's. Mom would put a mixture of sulfur and molasses all over us. Then we put our long handle underwear on, and go to bed. Needless to say we didn't smell too good. We lived on 38th street and Cedar Ave., by the railroad tracks. In 1928, my brother Everett and I would go over to the railroad tracks that winter and throw rocks at the steam engines as they went by. The firemen on the train would throw coal at us. They knew what we wanted. After a while we would have a peck sack full of coal, and go home. I remember the winter we had snow four feet deep and a snow drift that went clear over our roof.

That was the year Harry was teachers pet, as we perceived it. She would give Harry her fruit, an apple, banana, or an orange. Harry would give me the peelings. The banana skins were the worst. One day two policemen came to the house. They looked the place over, then took Harry and me with them. We were really scared, until they took us to a restaurant. We sat at the bar, and one of the policemen tossed a fifty cent piece on the counter and said, "fill em'up". Roast beef, Mashed Potato's, milk, and gravy. I can still taste it. I can still see us setting at that bar, two grubby white haired kids, shoveling food into their mouths. With two very tall policemen, one on each side of us, watching along with the other men at the bar eating to, and commenting about our appetites. This was probably the first full meal Harry and I had in a restaurant.

I didn't get a fair start in school in those days, as we didn't stay too long in one house. We would move every six months to a different neighborhood. I remember the fall of 1928. I was in, what we called 4A. My first day in the new school, my teacher gave us a spelling test. The words had been reviewed with the class before I arrived. Well naturally I failed the test. The teacher then put me back a half grade to 4B. I realized that English wasn't my best subject. I didn't think that was the right thing to do. Minneapolis schools were hard and opinionated in those days. It depended upon what side of the tracks you came from. I wasn't the smartest student in the class, but I was far from being the dumbest. What I needed was some good old fatherly direction and encouragement. I used to say to myself, "if I ever grow up and become a father, I'll be a father to my children if it's the last thing I do." I did the best with men teachers. The subjects I liked best were Botany, American History, Math, Algebra, and all of the manual training courses. Wood working, Machine shop, Mechanical Drawing, etc. My last year in school, somebody wasn't going to let me go any further. I would start a semester, and thought I was doing ok. When the report cards came out, I would get a failing mark in English and Math. The two subjects that would keep me from passing. Probably one of the reasons, I had so much trouble in high school. I didn't do my home work right. I didn't know how to put my Math problems down , with the correct structure. I could get the right answers to my problems, but they were graded also upon structure. I can remember that my sinus's gave me a lot of trouble that would prevent me from concentrating on my class work. If only I could get outside again and clear my nose. Part of my trouble was food and clothes. I was always hungry, and would often say, if only I could get enough to eat. I remember at school lunch, I had a nickel to spend, and I had to make a choice. A scoop of mashed potatoes or a candy bar. I wore the same pair of pants, shirt and shoes all year. They would get washed on weekends, and maybe ironed once during the week. There never was any food at home. When school was over, I would go down to lake Nokomis, and with my Bamboo fishing pole, catch a few Sun fish, Perch and Bass, take them home, and cook them, for my after school snack. During the winter months, I set snares for Rabbits, and with my sling shot, I would hunt for squirrels, birds, and maybe a pheasant. I would also go down to the Minnesota river and find a small brook. Cut a small straight stick about the size of an arrow shaft. Sharpen it, then put my hand into the water with the stick, and wait for a fish to swim by. Then drive the stick through the fish. Usually I got about a dozen Shad that way, they were delicious. In the spring when the Great Northern Pike were spawning. I would shoot them for a meal. I went out to the Fort Snelling rifle range and dug up the bullets from the bank behind the targets. I got a long 30-30 or 30-06. It was a copper jacketed lead bullet about a quarter inch in diameter. I would cut it into pieces a quarter inch long. With my sling shot, I didn't miss. Every week end in the fall and early winter we (my friend Leo Nystrom) would pull a few carrots and some potatoes from a farmers field, on our way out to the Minnesota river bottoms. Build a fire and make a Mulligan stew. The meat would be what ever we managed to shoot on our way out there. My friend Leo Nystrom, was just like me, we liked the same things. Both of us loved the out of doors, hunting, fishing, and trapping. We met when we were about eight years old, and were together all through our school years. We used to move every six months, either up town or out to what we called the "old berg" (34th Ave So.). Leo's family would do like wise. We also had pretty much the same attitude about girls. We were very romantic about them, and to us girls were angels, to be loved and respected. We tolerated them, but didn't let them interfere with our lives. All during our high school years, we talked about going to Alaska when we graduated from high school. In those days, college was out of the question for families like ours. However we could embark on camping trips. Some guys could get a canoe and with their supplies they would go up the Minnesota river where it joined the Red River of the North and go all the way to Hudson's Bay, Canada.

Leo was very good with his sling shot, he never missed. I've seen him shoot a bird right out of the air. We used to hitch hike to a place called Elk River, about thirty miles north of Minneapolis. We would take a blanket and a loaf of bread, maybe a can of beans. We would fish or shoot something to fill out our menu. We slept under a railroad bridge on the ground. Many times it would rain, and we would lay in our blanket soaking wet until morning. Then try to get a fire going to dry out. We were tough, and usually went off fishing long before our blankets were dry. The best times were around the camp fire in the evening. The train would go by, and we would speculate as to where the train was going. I thought that some day I would ride that train and find out where it went. Fishing that river like we did, we discovered a big large mouth bass. We thought, it was at least three feet long. One afternoon, Leo's brother Walter wanted to borrow my White Miller fly. I had caught a lot of Bass on that fly, and didn't want Walt to use it, as I knew he would lose it. His line and pole wasn't big enough to hold that fish. He took it and he lost his line and my fly. One day I was fishing for Northern Pike. I had already caught three of them, and had them on a stringer tied to my belt. I was standing in about four feet of water, the fish were right at my feet. I felt something around my feet, but was too busy fishing. Until I caught a nice Northern Pike, and was going to put him on my stringer. When I noticed that all I had left on my stringer was three heads off my fish. There right at my feet was a big snapping turtle. He was about three feet in diameter. I very carefully threw my pole ashore and reached down and picked up that turtle, and took him ashore. I turned him up side down and killed him. We had turtle for supper that night.

Elk River was a very beautiful place, with very large trees growing high over the river. The river was thirty to forty feet wide, and about four to six feet deep, where the water was slow moving. It also had areas where the water was fast with rapids and deep pools. We found the bass in the deep pools and the northern in the slower moving water.

We learned how to camp those days. The most important lesson was to keep a clean camp site. Why I say this, one time we took my friend Grey Jordan with us. He opened a can of potted meat, then threw the empty can over his shoulder into the grass. When I came up from the river, I stepped on the can and cut my right index toe, so that the tendon was severed. It bled all night.

In the morning we started for home. I couldn't walk very well or stand too long. I laid down by the side of the road. When a ride came by, I jumped up, only to have the driver step on the gas and drive away. It was a long day going home. We learned our lesson. Be careful who goes camping with you. We loved the out of doors, and camping.

How ever Mom had to work, she worked way up town. When fall came, she would have us move back up town, to some apartment. Then when spring came around the middle of March, even sometimes earlier, we would talk her into moving back out to the old "Berg", as we called it. We didn't have a car, so we moved our meager belongings on the street car. If you can imagine, Harry and I loading our steamer trunk on the street car and hold it in front of us, till we got out to the end of the line when we got off. We would make several trips like this every day until we had everything moved.

One time we moved out to a house on 28th street. The house didn't have a central heating system, Electricity, or plumbing. We stayed one night then moved to a small house on 34th Ave. South. We lived there for several years. I was thirteen when this happened. We didn't have internal plumbing then either, neither did any one else.

I was confirmed in a German Lutheran Church when I was fourteen. When I took my confirmation class, I had to go to church every Saturday morning for an hour or so. I was required to memorize The LORDS PRAYER, THE 23rd PSALM, and the APOSTLES creed. We were required to recite these in front of the church during Sunday service. Along with a couple dozen other questions on the bible. We had our picture taken and soon afterward I received a picture of not only of my self but also of my entire class. I still have that picture.

Harry L. Mathieson 1942

Louis R. Mathieson 1942

That spring, Leo Nystrom and I found a crows nest. There were four young crows, still in pin feathers. We took two, and I named mine Filbert. It was a female. She was very loving, and would sit on my shoulder, and coo and run her bill around my ear and through my hair. The bad part was, when she pooped, and a big glob of yellow and white gooey stuff ran down the back of my shirt. I fed her bread soaked in milk until she was old enough to eat from what ever was left over from the table. There was a garage next door. One day Filbert fell into a pail of drain oil. She was missing for a few days. When I found her soaked up with that black oil, and very sick. I washed her with soap and water, then fed her bread soaked with milk. She got better. During this time she collected all of her treasures, and placed them on my front door step. I thought she would go off to die. She came back and seemed to be better. There was a dog across the alley from us. He was ugly. The dog bit me once, while I was playing ball. After that I would shoot the dog with my sling shot, when ever he came near my house. The dog would chase my cat and crow, when I was away. I remember coming home, and finding the cat and crow on top of our Ice Box, side by side looking towards the door.

One day that fall, a lady came to my door, and wanted to buy my crow. I said, "no, you don't have enough money to buy my crow, she's my pet. The women persisted, all week she came, and pleaded with me. Her son was ten years old, and had been sick all summer. All he wanted was a crow. Finally, I gave in and let her take my crow on a Friday afternoon. I waited until Sunday afternoon to call on her, to see how my crow, was doing. Filbert died that Saturday night. She died of a broken heart. The woman said, the crow lost all interest in life, and wouldn't eat. She put the crow down cellar in the coal bin. Her son hadn't given the crow a second thought, upon coming home from the hospital. I didn't realize a birds life could be so fragile.

After the winter of 1930, when things were so bad. The people from our church, wanted my mother to let one of her son's go out on a farm in Grove City, Minn. The farmer out there needed help. My brother Everett was chosen. He seemed to be the frailest of the four boys. At thirteen years old, he went. The farmers wife was pregnant, and in July she had her baby. The baby lived about a month, and died with pneumonia. The rest of that summer Everett stayed near Mrs. Oval, the farmers wife, and worked in the kitchen. He learned the basics of farm cooking. He told me he hated to go out in the field to work. When Fall came, they talked him into staying with them. Everett wanted to come home, and felt that he was being abandoned by his family. I felt that he was getting a break, for now he would be getting three square meals a day, a chance to get an education, also a warm bed at night. He did get an education. Everett was always good in school, and he was always teaching me good grammar. The rest of us had to quit school, and go to work, so we could eat, and pay the rent.

My father died in March 1938. He was fifty eight years old, and he died of extreme alcoholism, although I didn't know him that well, or thought that he might ever become a father to me. It had a very devastating effect on me. In those days I missed a father. I used to say, that if I ever become a father, I will be a father to my children if its the last thing I do.

We went to his funeral, This was the first time I had ever seen a dead person. Harry and I learned, that we had a little money left to us, by our grand mother, Mathieson. It was held in a trust, by our aunt Jenny Muir. Jenny told us she would use that money to bury her brother, our father.

That evening I was depressed. There didn't seem to be much of a future left for me. My dreams of having a father were gone. I quit school and joined the C.C.C.'s. Everett was the first to leave home. Kenneth was next. He joined the C.C.C.'s and was sent up to "Toftie on Lake Superior. Now it was my turn, I was sent up to Effie, Minn. Harry was the last one left, and I figured he had a good chance to make it through high school, as he would have enough to eat.

My C.C.C. Co. 1722 Days

On the first day of April 1937, I found myself, and twenty other guys on a Great Northern passenger train going North to Duluth, Minnesota. It was cold in Duluth, and we were glad to board our next train to Grand Rapids, Minn. It was the Soo line, and the rickety old coach was rough, but warm. It had an old round coal stove in one corner at the end of the coach. There were a couple rough looking woodsmen on board also. There was only one passenger coach to the train. The other cars were freight cars. It was after dark when we arrived at Grand Rapids, Minn.

There were some C.C.C. guys waiting for us. We piled into a stake body truck with a canvas top, and headed north. We were very excited, and happy. This was a great experience for us. We sat on board seats

Harry and Louie 1989

Mom and Dad, Louie, Everett, and Kenny
In our back yard at 2740 25th Avenue South, Minneapolis, Minnesota

About 1923
*Back Row:
???, Kenny
Front Row:
Louie, Wayne*

Louis Mathieson
*On my confirmation day, 1935.
I was 14 years old.*

John (Dad), Everett, Ella (Mom)
*Our home 2740 25th Avenue South
Minneapolis, Minnesota*

Floyd Mathieson, my half-brother

Front:
Harry, Louie holding kitty
Back:
Harold Wasick, Clifford Anderson,
Carol Northcutt

My half-brother was a harvester.

John and Louie Mathieson
1922

The Henry Mathieson family
*Jennie Muir, Henry Mathieson,
John Mathieson, Frank Mathieson,
Emilie F. Bilberg Mathieson*

Kenneth Mathieson
*Tofte, Minnesota
Kenny was the first to join the CCC's. He lived in a tent at first. He used to write to me using Birch bark for writing paper.
He printed all of his letters. 1935*

The Ella Mathieson family
*Everett, Kenny, Mom, Louis,
Harry. 1934*

Company 1722 C.C.C.
Deer Lake, Minnesota
February 4, 1939

along the sides of the truck. The rest of us sat on the floor. We crowded close together to keep warm. The gravel road was dusty, rough, and cold. Soon we were coughing from the dust that seeped through the truck curtain. We had to go some 64 miles into the woods, before arriving at the camp, around eleven o'clock that night. We were given temporary quarters for the night.

The next morning we had breakfast, then went down to the supply office. There we received our GI issue of clothes, much the same way you would receive them if you were in the army. Except for the army dress shirts, pants, ties, shoes, etc. we also received work clothes, Boots (We called them Pacs), dungarees, army blankets, pillows, sheets, and a cot. We were instructed to buy a foot locker. The foot locker cost five dollars, which would be taken out of our pay next month. We were then assigned to our barracks. I had barracks seven, located on the outside perimeter, next to the woods.

After our noon meal, we went to the camp hospital for our physical, and a film on sex education, army style. One movie I'll never forget. It showed the various stages of gonorrhea, and syphilis. It had a profound effect upon my conduct through out the rest of my life.

Our pay at camp amounted to thirty one dollars a month. We sent twenty five dollars home, and kept six dollars for our selves.

I used to buy a carton (thirty bags) of Old North State smoking tobacco, for five cents a bag. You had to roll your own cigarettes. Also a box of wooden matches, the matches were of great value, as we worked in the woods, and would need them, to build a fire every day. If I remember right, we had to pay $1.50 a month to pay for our laundry. The laundry was picked up by some one, who lived nearby, washed our clothes and returned them the next day. A month is a long time and the money we had left was usually long gone by the end of the month. We had a good library, so we read a lot. We also had forestry school, in the recreation hall, Tuesdays and Thursdays. Our instructor was the camp forester Tony Lundquist. I listened to every word he said. He was my roll model, and I wished I could go back to school, and become a forester

Our first day at work started at seven on the work line. We had roll call. The barracks leader called us by name and assigned us to our work party, and which truck to get into. We were always anxious as to which truck we would be assigned to. This was important, as we knew which truck, or crew, did the various kinds of work. For instance, truck No. One, did road side clean up. That was a dirty job, and we didn't like it. Truck No. 2, was the logging crew. We liked that, because that crew was cutting virgin Norway pine trees. Some of these trees were three and four feet in diameter. We cut these trees with an eight foot long cross cut saw, and it took two men to pull the saw back and forth. We thought, this was man's work and we loved it. There was also the Saw mill crew, the road building crew, and camp maintenance. Although we had Bull Dozers, we had to load our dump trucks by hand. Shoveling gravel into the truck. I was doing that one day, when a bumble bee from the gravel bank struck me right between the eye's. The bee knocked me flat on my back. I thought I was hit by a baseball bat. I got up with two black eyes. Truck No. 6 was the survey crew, and Truck No. 7 was the reconnaissance crew, which was considered the best job in camp. It required considerable training.

My first job in camp was tree planting. It was the first of April and in that country an ordinary rain storm could turn into a snow storm. It was tough rugged work. We lined up, about twenty five guy's, mixing the seasoned men with the new kids. Our job was to tear a two foot square hole in the top two inches of roots and bushes. Then move on to the next spot, three or four feet further on. We did this with a five pound cutter mattock. This tool was heavy and the roots were like steel cables. Hazel brush was the worst. Our hands were soon raw with torn blisters, and our muscles were just as sore. If we lagged behind, the crew leader would be right behind us pushing. Come on guys keep going, it started to rain, and the rain turned to snow. I thought they would stop and take us back to camp. But, no, they said work harder and you'll get used to being wet, and the weather will no longer bother you. That was important as I would later learn. I would find myself and all of the other guys out working in all kinds of weather, cold or warm.

When the day's work was over, and we piled into an open body stake truck, with board seats along the sides, for our trip back to camp. The older guys started a water fight in the truck with our water tanks. These are the same tanks you carry on your back to fight fire with a manual pump, used to fight fire in the woods. If I was wet and uncomfortable when I got into the truck, I was wetter and colder then ever now. Because of the wind chill caused by the speed of the truck.

Tired, we'd pull into camp hungry as bears. First we had to clean up, shower and put some clean clothes on, and get ready for supper. This cleaning up was a very serious matter. We had one guy that wouldn't clean up or shower at all. We grabbed him and took him into the shower and scrubbed him with cold water and a scrub brush. He was red all over. A day or two later he left the camp.

We had plenty of good food, and at the supper table there was no talk, or horse play. We were told that in a logging camp, there was no talking at the table, and we figured we were the same as a logging camp, as our foremen were all retired lumber Jacks. We also learned table manners. I thought I would be able to return to my barracks and turn in, as I was exhausted. It didn't turn out that way. The older guys had to have their entertainment for the night. They had to hassle the new men. There were about four or five of us in my barracks. They wrestled us to the floor, took our clothes off, and smeared our tooth paste over our genitals' and then poured ink on to that. Then with no clothes on, we were instructed to run around outside the barracks several times. It was cold out there, and snow banks. If we were good natured about it, we were allowed back into the barracks. This usually lasted until around ten, or eleven o'clock at night. I used to wonder where these guys got all of their energy. We suffered this treatment through April and May, until Memorial Day weekend.

Memorial Day week end came and the camp provided us with a ride into Grand Rapids. We had to find our way back to camp three days later. There wasn't much traffic in those days. The people were sympathetic to C.C.C. guys. We had a ride if a car was going that way. Everybody seemed to stop at a little gas station, and lunch counter, on Lake Mille Lac's. It was the half way point on the 225 miles to Minneapolis. I remember the store had a slot machine. I put in a nickel and received fifteen cents. I bought a hamburger and a cup of coffee. In the back of the store, there was a round wood stove, with a circle of chairs. In the middle chair sat a young Indian girl. She sat very straight and looked straight ahead. I'll bet she didn't miss a thing that went on in that store.

We got home around eight PM. Naturally, I asked my mother for some money. The first thing she said to me was. "What are you doing home"? I told her they gave us Memorial Day off. I didn't get any money. To say the least I was very disappointed, and a little mad. I had seen Kenny my oldest brother, come home from the C.C.C. camp, and she gave him money. This was the end of the month, naturally she didn't have any money. I didn't say anything to her about that.

The next morning I got up early and hitched hiked back to camp. I had good rides and arrived in Grand Rapids around noon. Then I got a five mile ride out of town, and found myself on that hot dusty road to Effie, Minn., some sixty miles north. I walked all afternoon, and evening went into night. It was a dry, hot day. Somewhere on that road was a country store, and I stopped in. I asked the store owner for a drink of cold water. Some how he gave me a cold beer. The name of that beer was Golden Grain Beer. I shall never forget it. (It was cold and refreshing.) When you think about it, this beer was cooled by natural ice, and this store must have had an ice house near by. Any way It quenched my thirst.

As I walked along this road I could smell the scent from the pines and other forest smells. This was Memorial day week end and the song birds were singing as it was early spring up there. The Balsam and spruce trees give off a strong scent. Rotting wood and flowers. It was perfume to my nostrils, I loved it. Once in awhile a chipmunk or a squirrel would come out of the forest and scold me for getting to close to his home. As evening closed in, as the forest closed in over my head, the cheepers started singing. I felt very comfortable walking along this road and the coming darkness didn't bother me at all. All of these sounds I missed very deeply when I was out in Pearl Harbor two years later.

I walked all afternoon and evening. It was around three in the morning, and I was getting worried. I thought I wouldn't get enough sleep, and would be too tired to work in the morning. I passed through Effie, Minn. and was on the last fifteen miles, when a car stopped and picked me up. I squeezed in with the other guys coming back to camp. It was the last car going into camp that evening.

The next morning, one of the guys that had given me such a hard time all spring with his foolishness. He wanted to know why I was back in camp? He said, "I didn't think I'd ever see you again". Well now I had my chance, I told him. I liked it here in this camp, and I wasn't going to let a little shit like him drive me away, and I meant it. From then on he couldn't do enough for me. He would give me anything I wanted, if I asked. Only I was too proud to ask him for anything.

We started tree planting about the middle of May, and we planted for two weeks. Tree planting was easier and faster than scalping. At one time each man on my crew planted over a thousand tree's in one day. The tree's were about eight inches long, and they came wrapped in wax paper, and moss. We had a tray to put the trees in, with plenty of moss, which we kept well watered. We took the tree at the crown, between our two fingers. We had a long pole, (we called it a Jo bar) with a kind of spade at the end, and a place to put our foot to drive it into the ground. We drove this tool into the center of the scalp and into the ground, moved it forward and back, pulled it out, then inserted the tree roots into the ground, being careful to keep the crown level with the ground, and then drive the heel of our boot into the ground behind the tree. Then move on to the next scalp. During the tree planting season, every body in camp took part in this operation. The main reason we were up there in this camp was to plant trees.

Tree planting was over the first of June. We started new jobs. These were anxious times. We were all looking for new interesting jobs. For me I got road side clean up. It was a dirty wet cold Job. We had to pick up everything that laid on the ground, whether it was a stick or a log rotted or not we burned it, They were usually coated with ice and snow, and some times we had to brake the ice away to get it into the fire. It was still cold up there in the north country. I can recall seeing snow banks in the woods. That first day I had a sore throat, and I was beginning to wonder if this was such a good place after all. There wasn't much I could do, but stick it out, and hope for the best. The weather got better, and I soon got used to the hard work.

As luck would have it, I had been going to Forestry school all spring, when the opportunity came, I was ready. After the spring tree plant was over, the first of June. I had to work on the road side clean up crew for a few weeks. The first day of July it came. I was so afraid that I wouldn't make it. Who would believe, eight months later, I would be chosen to lead this crew, and also become a barracks leader. This was the top job in the camp. But, first I am getting ahead of myself.

The foremen in this camp were old timers, and were used to hard work themselves. They used to tell me about the virgin pine timber they cut twenty years earlier. The man in the black and white checkered shirt, told me these stories. He said he would cut two and three million board feet of pine in a winter. Then drive it down the Big Fork river. He's the one that told me how his brother died. Some of the log drivers had gone into town the night before, and got drunk. They told stories about a town called Craigville, which was located just north of Effie about five miles. It was made up of twelve buildings. Eight whore houses and one steam bath and a barber shop. Of course the whore houses served liquor. There were a lot of story's about these people. They were made up of Swedes, Finns, Norwegians, and Indians. How they would get drunk and there would knife fights and who ever lost was thrown in to the river. One story was about a dynamite stick thrown in to the river and it killed all of the fish below the dam. They had a log jam on the river the next day. His brother carried a stick of dynamite out there, and put it under the key log. Then lit the short fuse. The man behind him had been out all night and he was too slow moving back to shore. The blast killed his brother.

Finally, my day came, and I started on reconnaissance. You can't imagine how I felt. Just to get off that road side clean up crew. Now I could tolerate this place again. I was to be a compass man. I had to count my paces, and stay on a course. We had a declination of four degrees from true north, and true south, and had to come out to within six feet from our designated point one mile away. We had to know at any point along the trail, where we were, and put it down on our map. We drew lines that marked the different timber growths, and streams, tree diseases, topography, and types of soil. We knew the soil type by the trees that grew there. If there was a stand of trees that were merchantable, by that, we measured the diameter of the tree's trunk and if they were over six inches at the top we considered this plot as a merchantable. We counted the trees, and measured them into board feet. We did this with a tool that would calculate the trees heights, using trigonometry formulas we learned in high school. We measured the trees diameter. Sometimes we drilled a core, that would tell us the trees age. All this data would be transferred to a large map in the forestry building. There was around twelve crews, out all doing the same thing.

Everybody's maps had to match, on the big map. A township is six miles square. It was divided into sections, each one mile square. That made thirty six sections. Each section was broken down to sixteen forty acre maps. We had a survey crew, that ran the survey lines, and some times we ran survey lines. The survey crew set the five and fifteen chain stakes that we used as our starting points for entering the forest. We went one mile north to the five chain stake on the northern end of that section. Then we would go East on this line to the fifteen chain stake, and then south to the other fifteen chain stake. That was our days work. Some times we were through our days work by three o'clock in the afternoon, and then on other days we could be working well into the night time.

The hardest part of this job was to plunge into the forest. The brush and tree limbs would tug at our clothes and the same thing would slow our steps. It was hard work to go thru the thick under brush. If we came to a stream or river we waded it. I remember one time in the early spring, crossing the little Fork river on ice flows. A very hazardous thing to do. I had a pair of tall leather boots. The boats reached clear to my knee's. The toes were worn out, and I nailed the toe down, and bent the nails over. The boots were two sizes larger than my foot. The main idea was to keep the sticks and stones out of the shoe. The high tops were good as they kept the brush from rubbing the skin from my shin bone. On the soles of these boots, I had spikes screwed into the soles. Leather can get very slippery in the woods. We had crossed this river not more than an hour or so before, On solid ice. Now we were on our way back. There wasn't time to consider the place to cross. As there was nothing but woods north to the Canadian border. The river was breaking up, and I had to move fast. I started out, on large ice flows, but out in the middle the ice broke up into smaller pieces, and the river was picking up speed. I took a chance and ran and stepped on the smaller chunks. Each chunk dipped in the water as I ran. The hardest part of these days came with the spring melt. With all that snow melting, we found ourselves walking in ice cold water all day long. We couldn't keep our feet dry. We were very healthy those days. I never had a sick day, no matter how bad the going was. We finished our day's work. The next day we went on to another job.

Another time I came upon a stand of young trees so thick I had to climb them, and bend them to pass through. This sounds easy, but going through them, I wondered how far I could get, I knew the trees could get bigger and then I couldn't bend them to get through. I felt trapped, and it took a lot of discipline to keep going. Another time, I crossed a stream on top of the snow. The snow gave way and I found myself up to my waist in the middle of the stream, with only my head sticking out above the snow. My partner had to pull me out. The temperature was about ten degree's below zero. We had to build a fire on the spot. While I stood near the fire and turned to keep warm on both sides. My partner rung my clothes out, and half dried them on a stick near the roaring fire. I put my clothes on half dry, and continued on with my days work.

Another morning we were snow shoeing four or five miles along a trail going north to our most remote section. I was first in line. As I went along, I would brush the snow off the bushes, with a stick about thirty inches long so as to keep the snow off my neck. I reached forward to knock the snow off a bush in front of me, and I was face to face with a Canadian lynx. I had reached forward so far that my face was within a foot from the ground. His mouth was just a few inches from my face. I remember well his wide red mouth, and large teeth. I was lucky, as I surprised him. He was waiting for me. For a split second we made eye contact. The cat seemed to explode, as snow went every where. You could see a puff of snow every fifteen feet or so, as he ran down the trail and out of sight. I can still remember those green eyes and red mouth, with that little tuft of hair above each eye. This type of contact seemed to be the most dangerous in the woods up there. We met an old Trapper one day. He warned us to never travel alone in the woods. As the most likely danger would be a Bob Cat jumping down onto your back. This old trapper was a little crazy, he had a laugh like a witch. But he also had several dead Bob Cats slung over his shoulder.

The forest itself can be a very dangerous place to be in also. On a windy day we could hear loud crashes every so often. Back about 1917, a saw tooth beetle infestation took place in those woods. This beetle killed the old growth Tamarack trees. Now some twenty years later the rot was taking place around the root crown and on a windy day, these trees would come crashing down.

The trees would make excellent fire wood for our kitchen stoves, with their straight grain, and cedar like wood. On Saturdays I worked for the Army. They had me doing work around camp. During the winter, I chopped fire wood for the kitchen stoves. I chopped this wood into pieces not more than 3 inches thick and sixteen inches long. All day long I chopped. When the day was done I had a pile of wood as big as my house. I would grab that axe by the handle half way up and chopped with one hand as the other hand would turn the log exactly three inches. I had a muscle on my wrist that stood up a good half inch. I was in excellent health, and didn't seem to ever get tired.

During the months of November, December, and January, it seemed to me that it snowed every day. If not it snowed some part of the day. The snow depth increased to a record seven feet. Then when February came in, the temperature went down and stayed down, all month the temp. was never warmer than ten degrees above zero, and it went down to forty nine degrees below zero. We didn't have to work, until the temp. got up to twenty degrees below zero. The forestry superintendent would go over to the thermometer and put a lighted match under it, and raise the temp. up to twenty below, or better. Then call the camp doctor, for permission to send the men out. To look at this from his point of view, it went like this. If he had waited for the temp. to raise gradually with the sun. The time would be around twelve noon, or one o'clock. Then, there wouldn't be enough time left in the day to get any work done.

It was just one of these days. The night before, we had a big snow fall, about eighteen inches. We started out and found that we had to push the truck, the fifteen or more miles into the woods. There was around twenty five or six of us in this crew. We were going to cut a survey line that day. When we got in there, the truck ran out of gas. Tony Lundquist, our foreman asked for a volunteer to walk out to the road and find a telephone and call the camp for somebody to bring us out some gas. I volunteered. I felt that I didn't want to cut survey line that very cold day. I took a lunch, and I carried my canteen with water, and my cruising hatchet on my belt. I cut a small club about thirty inches long. I would use that if I got into trouble with some wild animal. I walked the road for a while then took off across country, I felt confident, that I knew the lay of the land, and it was much more comfortable walking in the woods instead of the road. The road made too many turns, and this way it was shorter. I walked all afternoon and came out on the main road around three o'clock in the afternoon, just as the sun was going down. About two O'clock that day a pack of wolves picked up my trail, and followed me, at times they were almost within the reach of my club. I think there were five of them. They followed just to my rear and on each side of me. Like a dog will do to you, when you walk along the street. They couldn't get very close because my snow shoes would kick them in the throat as I lifted my foot for each step forward. They were not afraid of me, and when I came out to the road at dark, they got real brave and followed me right down the road. Because I had taken my snow shoes off. At times I had to turn and face them, and try to hit one of them with my club. At one time, I almost threw my club at one of them, I didn't because if I did they would have been all over me. It didn't take long to get pitch black. With all that white snow around I was able to see in the dark. I went to the first home, and they said their phone was disconnected. I went down the road another mile. This house also said their phone didn't work. The last house that I knew of was about three or four miles further down the road. The wolves were getting on my nerves, I had to turn and face them every so often now. I reached this last house and they said their phone didn't work either. I told them there was a crew of men some fifteen miles in the woods and our truck was out of gas, and they were waiting for me to send for help. I also told them I had to come in as there was a pack of wolves out in the road waiting for me, and they had been trailing me all day. They let me in to their house. It was a small house, two rooms and they were around sixty years old. They could see that I was a young kid, so they offered me some soup and then a piece of Blueberry pie. I asked if I could use their telephone, I called camp, and they sent a truck out to get me. Although this was about eight o'clock in the evening, The driver told me the camp figured we would be out of gas and had sent a truck with some gas, about the same time I had come out of the woods that day.

One day I was going through the woods and came upon a dead deer. It was standing up in a big bush. It had broke through the deep snow and became lodged in the Hazel bush, and starved to death. The deer's feet couldn't touch the ground, and the deer couldn't shake himself out of there.

Along about the same time this happened, we had to reach out to the furthest section that was in our township. We went the fifteen miles into the forest. Then we had to walk north five miles, and east three miles, to get to where we would start our days work. Half way there, it started to snow. It was coming down pretty thick. This was the day

I run into the Canadian Lynx, I had to brush the snow off the branches. We started in and I soon had to light a match and hold it under my compass, as the needle was sticking. I was using my matches up. I told my mapper, (Kit Gustafson) that I would have to take a sighting on three trees in line, and make our return trip back, sighting three trees as I went. In a situation like this you can't take your eyes off from those trees, if you, did you would lose them instantly. I made it back to within six or eight feet from the fifteen chain stake. This was one days work that we didn't want to repeat, and I was relieved, when we came out so well, in spite of the storm.

On our way back to the truck, we had to cross a Muskeag about a mile wide. When we started to cross it, we couldn't see more than a few feet as it was snowing so hard, and our old tracks were covered up. I suggested that we go along the edge of the Muskeag, but Kit said we could feel our way by our old snow shoe tracks. It worked, we crossed the Muskeag, and walked right into our trail in the woods.

These days were long and some times we didn't get in to camp till long after supper. It was one of these days, when the truck broke down and we were faced with a two or three hour wait for the camp to send some body out to get us. We would need a lot of fire wood to keep twenty five guys warm.

There was a big white pine tree along side of the road, that had been hit by lighting some time in the past. It looked like a good source of fire wood for the fire we would need. I dug the snow out from behind the tree and slid in the hole, to start the cross cut saw going. Ray Lukenbill our leader, was on the other end of the saw. The tree was about three feet in diameter. We had the cut almost through, and we had the notch all cut to lay the tree down along side of the road. When about three quarters of the way up the tree. The tree broke off and started down on top of me. I tried to get out, but slipped back. I was trying to get to one side as the tree was coming down on top of me. Ray reached in and grabbed me by my coat collar and dragged me out just in time. WHEW, I thought I'd had it. We cut the rest of the tree up, and had a roaring fire going. We didn't get back in camp until around midnight. There is so much to say about my experiences up here in the north woods. Every day was a challenge.

We usually tried to wait until most of us were out of the woods, when we ate our lunch. In order to spend so much time out there in the woods and stay warm. We built a small lean-to for a shelter. We made this shelter out of the Balsam trees that were so abundant there. We picked two Balsams about seven feet apart, and of the same size, also about four inches in diameter. We cleaned the branches off about five feet high. Then cut two poles about seven or eight feet long and laid them against our two trees, with one end laid over a branch so as to hold it up. Then we cut several poles and laid them across these two poles, and then wove Balsam branches between them for our roof. We then laid a log down in front of the two trees, and then laid Balsam bows in back of this log for a bed. In front of all this we built a fire. We were very comfortable here, and were able to rest until we were picked up by our truck. Walking on snowshoes in the woods and the brush, our legs got very tired. I used to have terrible leg cramps in the night after a long walk the day before.

During our lunch time the Canada Jays, "we called them Whiskey Jacks", would land on our shoulders and arms, and slide or walk down our arms to our hands and eat our sandwiches. One time they actually pecked bread out of my mouth. We loved these birds and wouldn't harm them in any way. One night we had to wait for one crew to come out of the woods, as they had along walk that day. It was long after dark, when the truck picked us up, it was around ten thirty at night. Instead of going back to camp we went deeper into the woods.

There we found a bull dozer stuck, out in a bog. With all that snow on the ground, it was hard to know what kind of ground was under the snow. I cut a long slender pole about twenty feet long and pushed it down a hole next to the bull dozer, and couldn't touch bottom. The only thing that was holding that bull dozer up was the frozen network of roots made by the Labrador tea. We cut these long Tamarack poles into ten foot lengths, and made a corduroy road under it. We looked like a bunch of dwarfs lugging these big trees from the forest, down to this giant orange machine out in the middle of this bog. The forestry superintendent told us never drive over ground that had cat tails growing on it. We couldn't see any cat tails as the snow was to high. We waited until the larger bull dozer from camp arrived, and pulled it out. We didn't get into camp until after midnight.

We got through the month of March some how, it wasn't very pleasant. Some days the sun would come out and spring would be in the air. On a warm spring day in the woods, the fresh air, with the cent of the pine trees, is the sweetest perfume that I have ever experienced. Two years later, when I was in the Navy out in Pearl Harbor, I was very home sick for this smell. The first part of April we started Scalping again, and then the tree planting season. During this time, some body in camp found a Birch bark canoe. He found the canoe sunk in a stream at the outlet of Big Deer Lake, With a big rock in the middle of it. The Indians from the Net Lake Indian reservation had made it, they probably used it to go into the town of Craig. I used this canoe in my spare time. I loved to go fishing out in Big Deer lake.

One day I was fishing, and noticed a deer swimming out in the middle of the lake. It was windy and a chop was going. I noticed the deer would make three efforts to swim forward, then fall back two, and it seemed to be swimming in a circle. I came up closer and herded it straight toward shore. At times it seemed to give up, and I would have to slap the water with my paddle, to keep it going. When I was near shore, I called to some guys to grab the deer when it landed. The deer was exhausted, and when it came ashore it collapsed in a heap on the shore. The guys held it down, until we got a stretcher, and loaded her on to it. The front leg had been shot off, and was hanging by the skin. We took it up to our ball field, and our camp doctor amputated the leg at the knee. The next day we released it. It stayed near our camp. That next winter you could see the three foot prints in the snow. We called her Peg Leg.

I used this canoe every chance I got. I had more fun. I found these streams that came into Big Deer Lake, and I would follow them, through the woods to other lakes. The fishing was fabulous. I loved Battle Lake. To get there, I had to cross Big Deer Lake, then a stream into pickerel lake, cross that lake to another stream, which wound through the woods about three or four miles, and came out to Battle lake.

One Sunday afternoon, I decided to take the canoe and go fishing. I made the trip to Battle Lake and as I came out into the lake, I thought I would go over to the other side of the lake. The shore line over there was Muskeag and spruce trees. It looked like the forest had grown out over the shore of the lake. I imagine the water at the edge of the shore was about twenty or more feet deep. I got within 30 feet of the shore and made one cast. My lure, (a red and white dare devil). My lure landed just short of the edge of the shore, and I let it sink. When I retrieved it. I thought I had hooked on to some slime on the bottom. As the lure got closer, I could see that, there was a big fish following it. The fish was so big that it startled me, and I lifted my line and lure up over my head, and the line and lure landed on the other side of the canoe. The fish, a big Musky, came up and over my right shoulder. He was at least three or four feet long, and I would estimate a good forty pounds. It scared me. If the fish had landed in the canoe, he would have destroyed it. I very quickly paddled back across the lake. This side of the lake was on higher ground with some big trees and a nice sand beach. I fished across the outlet to this stream and caught three nice six to eight pound Walleyed Pike. Then I started back to camp, arriving after dark around nine or ten o'clock. My assistant barracks leader, was also a camp cook. I asked him to cook up my fish, which he did, and several of us had a late night fish fry.

After awhile I got pretty good with that canoe and could paddle it rather expertly. (My paddle was carved out of an old pine board). I was coming through the stream from Pickerel lake one Sunday afternoon, and just before coming out into Big Deer Lake. I spotted a girl in the woods, in a little clearing, she was going to take her clothes off, and put her swim suit on. I felt a little embarrassed, I couldn't stop, so I kept my head down and paddled very softly by her, respecting her privacy. I passed by her, just a few feet away, and just under the bank where she was. I came out into Big Deer Lake, just as she was coming out also. She hollered to me, and wanted to know if I had watched her change clothes. I replied, no. I told her, I kept my head down and didn't look at her. She then asked me to take her for a boat ride. I said I couldn't as I had been away all day, and didn't want to miss supper.

It was about this time of year. I came in from work, and as usual the reconnaissance crew was late. I was crew leader and barracks leader now, and was a respected old timer. Some of the men in my barracks were new, and from the city, and not knowing the ways of wild life. They had come across a fawn deer hiding in the brush. These guys were scalping, in preparation for tree planting. One of the new men picked up this deer, before the crew leader could tell him not to. They brought the fawn into camp. The guys had built a small cage in back of my barracks. Then had gone out to some cottages on the lake and managed to find a baby bottle. They were attempting to feed this deer. But with six big guys standing over it. The fawn was petrified, with fear.

After a while they came into the barracks discouraged. They came over to my bunk and asked me if I knew how to feed that fawn, and would I help them. It was already around nine thirty that evening. I said, "Give me the bottle of milk, and I'll see what I can do". As I went out the door, I scooped up a little kitten one of the guys in my barracks had. She was a small black and white five week old kitten. I told these guys to stay inside as I didn't want to scare the fawn any more than it already was. I sat out back by the cage and played with the kitten for quite some time. After a while the kitten noticed the deer, and went in to touch noses. Then it came out to me. I took the milk and put some milk on the kittens nose and sent it back to the deer. The little deer seemed to turn it's head in my direction. I reached out as far as I could and slipped the bottles nipple into the deer's mouth. The deer took it, and in a moment the bottle was dry. The little deer started to bleat for more. I had to go into the barracks and wake up the camp cook, to get some more milk. The next morning the camp cook was shaking me at three AM to get up and feed that deer. I had to do this for about a month. Then the kitchen crew gave me a break and took over my duties. That fawn deer was the cutest, with the little kitten they were together all of the time. She didn't forget me either. If I went some where she would follow me. If I sat down on the lawn by some barracks to chat with the guys. That deer would come up behind me and touch me on the neck or ear with her nose, ever so gently. I was the one that the deer seem to bond to, even though the kitchen crew took over my duties of feeding her after a few weeks went by. I was away most of the time so I never really kept tract about how she tolerated the other guys. I tried to act nonchalant and never reveal my love for this animal. I was a crew leader and these guys would take advantage of me if they found out I was soft.

I left this camp that fall of 1939, and enlisted in the U.S. Navy in the spring of 1940. In the years that followed, I used to wonder how my little deer was getting along up there in that big woods. Five years went by and I was in the navy's advanced diesel school, in Cleveland, Ohio, as an instructor, in G.M. diesel engines. One day, after lecturing to my class for fifty minutes. It was our routine to take a ten minute coffee break. Instead of going down to the instructor's room, I stayed in my room to work on some test papers when, I noticed a small group of sailors down in the back of the room talking. I kept hearing the word "Charlie Black, did this and that." Then I listened and learned that this sailor was talking about a deer hunt he had been on. I went back there and eves dropped. When I was sure he was talking about Effie, Minnesota. I tapped him on the shoulder and ask him if he was talking about Big Deer lake Minnesota, and about my pet deer Effie. He said yes, how did you know about that. I said he was talking about me, and did this Charlie Black shoot the other deer, the three legged one. He said "no, ole peg leg" was too smart for him. We were amazed that after five years and so many miles away, I discovered what happened to my pet deer. I was heart broken to find out how my little deer died, and also I thanked GOD for letting me know what happened. I was and still am very sentimental about this story.

Whenever I sent my crews out on reconnaissance. I always took the most difficult and furthest day's work to map, as I was always afraid something might happen.

About the first of September we were called out one Sunday afternoon to fight a forest fire. I was concerned about going in to the forest to fight a fire at this time of day. As we road along I mentioned to a guy about a cloud over to the north West. He came back with, "That ain't no rain cloud that's smoke from a fire we were going to."

We entered into six weeks of fighting forest fires. We were on the work line at four a.m. in the morning, and we worked until midnight, every day.

About five weeks in to fighting fire we were to have a day of rest. About ten O'clock that morning we were called out. Because of an emergency. A farm house was in jeopardy. The farm was about a mile in from the road. As we were running down the road to the farm house, about a mile away I couldn't help but notice the slash along side of the road. It was piled high and about a hundred feet on each side of the road, and the slash was brown so I knew when it caught fire it would burn fast. When we got to the farm house we turned to with a water bucket and from the well we threw the water on the roof of the barn. When the fire hit the slash. The flames were over a hundred feet high, and a solid wall of flame. On the other side of the farm the fire was racing up a huge swamp area, and the sound was like a thousand steam engines roaring towards us. We tried to keep the barn roof from catching fire. We soon drained the well dry, we tried throwing dirt on the roof. The fire soon got ahead of us, and we had to go into the house, as everything outside was catching on fire. We were only in the house a few minutes and we could go back outside, as the fire had gone by. The roof on the house was on fire, so we threw dirt on the house to put out the fire. A water truck came in threw the fire, and we were then able to put the rest of the fire on the house out. The barn was completely gone by then. We had turned the horses and cattle loose before the fire came through, and amazingly they were still alive, but minus some hair. This fire was traveling in the tree tops, and going thirty five miles and hour. This was in the fifth week of fighting fire, and all of us were very tired. This was supposed to have been a day of rest for us.

We only got to sleep in till ten o'clock that morning. We usually fought the fire until sun down. Then walk the fire line until midnight. Then return before sun up in the morning, to stay in control during the day. Only to have the wind come up during the day and jump the fire line. We worked very hard during this time of the day. One day I was cutting pine tree's as fast as I could to get ahead of the fire, when the fire over took me. The smoke was so thick, I had to hit the ground, and with my nose right on the ground I managed to back out of that area.

The parts I remember the best. When our truck would arrive with fresh coffee and our lunches. They brought plenty of food. Sometimes I would eat three lunches. That's two sandwiches, a cookie, and an orange or apple. The sandwiches were, one cheese and one beef, or ham. Some times peanut butter and jelly. I rolled my own cigarettes. My tobacco was Bull Durham, or Old North State. I liked Old North State best.

It started to snow the first day of November and the fire was out. By the middle of November we had two feet of snow on the ground. Deer hunting season started, and we started our deer check stations. Because of the remoteness of the area, we had to keep track of the hunters going into the forest. It was a volunteer operation. I had the six PM. to six AM. shift. We were on a remote road going into the forest. Our station consisted of an old Army tent with a barrel stove, and stove pipe going out the front side of the tent. Then a hundred feet in back of the tent was our toilet. A log laying over a depression in the ground, still a very necessary part of the camp. We had kerosene flares in front of the tent, and one hundred fifty feet down the road on each side, with appropriate signs, indicating all hunters must stop and register. My partner was Grey Jordan. We had joined together, and had been friends from the time we were ten years old. Grey always had to go to the toilet, when we arrived at our station. One night he was out back. I could hear the wolves howling nearby. The next thing I knew, Grey came charging up to the tent hanging on to his pants, hollering for me to open the tent flap, as the wolves were hot on his heels.

Our biggest problem during those cold nights, was to stay warm. The stove seemed to die out. I took some paper and fresh kindling wood to start a fresh fire, only to have the smoke come back at me. The smoke filled the tent, driving us out side. The temperature out side was around fifteen or twenty degree's below zero. I noticed, no smoke coming out of the chimney. I grabbed the stove pipe and took it apart. It was filled with frozen smoke, or should I say soot. I cut a pole and reamed the pipe out and put it back together again. We soon had a roaring fire going. We blamed the trouble on punky wood.

With the fire going good now, we could hear the steady sizzle of the snow flakes as they hit the hot stove pipe. The tent began to warm up, and I soon became sleepy. In order to stay awake, I played my mouth organ. I knew one tune, "Pack up your troubles on an old gray mare, and ride away, ride away." I forget how the words went. I also tried to play Deep Purple, only I wasn't very good at it.

With night fall the temperature would fall twenty to thirty degrees below zero. Then with out warning—crack! The sound resembled a rifle shot. But at two or three o'clock in the morning, it was very unlikely that anybody would be out hunting. The forest was silent now, earlier the Wolves or Coyotes were barking or howling. I never could distinguish the difference between them. I know some were timber Wolves as I had seen them take a Deer down and rip it apart. Then the flares down the road would go out. We would have to take out the spare flare fill it and light it. The next problem, who was going to take it down the cold road and exchange it. We usually waited till just before we were to be relieved. Although the weather was cold with fresh north west winds, I can still remember the acrid smell of burnt wood from the forest fires. In two weeks we didn't see a hunter, we didn't see anybody. It snowed every day, and when the deer hunt was over, we went back to reconnaissance. We started wearing snow shoes.

My life up there in that C.C.C. camp was tough, and interesting. I loved it, and never gave any thought about holidays, except Christmas, Thanksgiving, Memorial Day, and the Fourth of July. In the time that I was up there I came out of the woods twice. The first time was on Memorial Day, and the second one was on my eighteenth birthday. My birthday falls on Dec. 19, and up there it wasn't safe to leave camp unless you had a ride. I had been working for the Captain's wife on Saturdays that fall. She was from Alabama, and had a very sweet southern accent. I loved to hear her talk. I suppose for her living way up in that northern woods she was quite lonely. We soon were good friends. I think she found out, that I hadn't been home for a long time. The camp offered to provide a truck to take us to Grand Rapids for a weeks leave. I wasn't going as the walk back was too risky for this time of year. The captain called me into his office, and told me to go home. He would make arrangements to meet me in Grand Rapids on the following week end. He gave me a telephone number to use to contact him, and he would give me a ride back to camp. His name was Captain L.R. Moody.

I was home for my eighteenth birthday, and I was looking for this day as I had a small inheritance coming to me. We went to my aunt Jenny Muir's house, to make arrangements to receive this money. After a long wait, we went down to the bank. I signed some papers, and I received around eighty dollars. I was told to buy some Savings bonds, so as not spend all of that money at once. Which I did. I bought three twenty five dollar bonds for eighteen dollars and seventy five cents. I took the rest of the money with me. My aunt took the bonds and kept them in her savings box, at the bank. That left $23.75 for me to spend for Christmas, and also some money for the rest of my vacation. That's the most money I ever had at one time in my life. I had a grand time.

My friend Bill Plate arranged for a blind date for me, at this girls house. We sat and talked in the girls living room, with the girls mother and her friend in the next room. The girls played a favorite record, and we were to dance. They got me on the floor, but when I got close to that girl, I couldn't understand what happened to me, but I had to get away from her. I went out to the kitchen shaking all over. I was embarrassed and red as a beet. I wasn't used to those kind of feelings, and I wouldn't allow myself to experience that kind of luxury. I had to go back up into the woods, and that would be too heavy a load to carry up there. I guess that's what I thought. I was confused, looking at it now I can understand. I was all right up there in the woods with out thinking about girls all of the time. I had to keep my mind clear as the work was too demanding to have anything else on it. We made some pop corn, after a little while we left and went home. I remember when I went into that house, the girls made a remark, that I had a fresh pine tree smell about me. Probably that's why that girl got too close to me for my comfort.

My vacation over, I hitch hiked my way back to Grand Rapids. It was late when I got there, and wondered if the captain would still be there when I called. It was around eight or nine o'clock in the evening. To my relief they were there, and we were soon on our way back to camp.

We didn't have a radio in my barracks, I believe if we had a radio the signal would have been too weak that far up in the woods. In those days T.V. was unheard of. We got our news by word of mouth. The guys that went into town once in awhile, would give us the news. That following summer, we heard about the Germans, and the Gestapo, and how they would go into peoples homes at night, and take them away to a concentration camp. We learned that the concentration camp was an awful place., it was worse than any prison we had. It was scary to me, as when I went to bed, I was vulnerable in my sleep. Then when Germany invaded Poland, that did it. Knowing we were in the army on the week ends. I thought, if there was a war, we would be the first to go. One of my friends was looking at a U.S. Navy brochure with a bunch of sailors standing around a swimming pool. It had a caption which read "Sailors are physically fit. We discussed what it was all about. I was very up set now, and needed to think about it.

I went down to the lake, and got into my canoe, and took off across the lake to Pickerel lake, then up stream to Battle Lake. There was a nice clearing just as you entered the lake. I could set and think here, and look out over the water. A pair of Loons were talking back and forth, and the water was smooth. It was the end of the day, (Sunday). I now knew I would have to leave this place, and it wasn't going to be easy. I realized that war was on the horizon, with a lot of danger. I wanted to survive the war. I realized I didn't have enough education, and I was lacking time. The next day I requested separation from the C.C.C.'s. I also requested the camp officers to request permission from the Minneapolis board of education to allow me to reenter high school. Grey Jordan, my friend also requested the same, and we left together.

i started the fall semester late and I had a hard time trying to catch up to my class. I didn't do to well, my brother Harry was now in the same grade. He would help me with my math lessons. By spring I decided I had better enlist in the U.S. Navy, and get some training before the war started. I was sworn in on the 20th of May 1940.

My U.S. Navy Days

In the spring of 1940, I went down to the U.S. Naval recruiting office, and after a preliminary medical exam, the recruiting officer swore us in. I forget just how it was done. I do remember, I had a lump in my throat when I signed my name on that enlistment form for six years. From that time on I was in the US Navy. What got me interested in the US Navy, was a brochure that was given to me, showing a bunch of sailors in swimming trunks, around a pool, and also a picture of a gym. Sailors were physically fit, the brochure said, and I liked that.

We boarded a train that night. I don't remember how many there were of us new recruits. In the morning we were rolling along the shore of lake Michigan, and I can remember seeing my first large ship. It was an iron ore collier. Upon arriving at the Great Lakes Naval Training center, we were brought into a room with a hundred other guys, and we were sworn in again. Then we were given a more thorough medical exam, and immunization shots. Next we had our hair cuts. Everybody had their hair shaved off. They claimed that there were germs, and mites, etc. in our hair. So they did this to protect our health. Next we entered the supply store. We had to remove all of our civilian clothes, put them in a box, to be shipped home. I never saw those clothes again. We were naked for the rest of the day. As we filed through the supply store. The store keepers loaded us up with our uniforms. We were measured for every item of clothing. When we finished we assembled in a large room, like a gym. There we were instructed to form a circle. The chief pharmacist mate instructed us, how to wear our uniforms, starting with our under wear. Then we were taught how to roll our clothing, and tie each item with a cord. Each item had to be of a certain size. When finished, our sea bag could be packed with our complete set of uniforms in a ship shape manner. Doing it this way, we could have a change of uniform out of our sea bag and each item of clothing would come out just as if it had been pressed or ironed. Our pants and jumpers were stored inside out and tied in a roll. All of this was done according to our Blue Jackets Manual. If you didn't roll your undress jumpers, and put them away in this manner. When you took them out of your sea bag, they would look horrible.

We also received our service number. Mine was 328 69 44. We were instructed to memorize it. I was nineteen years old, and there were one hundred men in my company. Some how I was given a second class petty officers rating, with a square knot insignia. I was to lead my company where ever we went. I carried our company flag. When our boot training was over, I went back to apprentice seaman.

Our first four weeks, we were in quarantine. We spent most of our time

Co. 1722 Effie, Minnesota
February 1939
Coming up from breakfast on a Sunday morning.

Below left: Louis Mathieson. We are in back of Barracks #4. That corner of the barracks you can see, is where I sat with "Effie" our pet deer and coaxed her to eat, later that summer.

Below right: Grey Jordan. We grew up together and signed up for the C.C.C.s at the same time. We have been lifelong friends.

These pictures are all that I have from negatives found after the war. All of the original photos were lost onboard the USS Oklahoma, December 7, 1941.

Left Photo:
Our Rec. Hall. We could play ping pong and pool. Also a library.
We held Forestry school here two nights a week, Tuesday and Thursday nights.

Bottom Left:
49 degrees below zero. Our showers and water tank are on the right side
of the picture. I often wondered why the water didn't freeze in the tank.
Sometimes the smoke froze up in our chimneys and drove us out into the cold.

Bottom Right:
Inside of Barracks Seven on a Sunday afternoon. We usually played cards or read. There
were no radios or TVs in our barracks.

Company 1722 C.C.C. Deer Lake, Effie, Minnesota – February 4, 1939

Doing reconnaissance on snowshoes. Notice the fence posts, my partner is on the left. I took the picture.

*We got a lot of satisfaction from it.
My partner's name as I remember them.
Kit Gustafson, I don't remember the other guy's name.*

*Bottom Left:
Emerine Peterson, and Dwight Spurgeon. I met Spurgeon the night before the attack, in the Army & Navy YMCA in Honolulu. He was a marine and was quite frightened.*

*Bottom Right:
Miller. He was from Minneapolis.*

Louis Mathieson
As I came out of the woods the day I had to climb the trees to squeeze through them. Summer 1939. Note how the knees of my pants are worn, tramping through the brush.
Co. 1722 Effie, Minnesota

*"Effie" – Our camp mascot.
Free to come and go as she pleased.*

*Kenny and Louie downtown Minneapolis the first day or so after leaving the CCC's.
1939*

marching and changing our uniforms, and learning how to sleep in a hammock. It was quite a trick to jump into the hammock and slide down in between the blankets with out rolling out the other side onto the deck. I didn't have any trouble, but some of the other guys did. We would have surprise inspections, and we would have to lay out our sea bags, with our clothes all rolled into neat little bundles. We also had our Blue Jackets manual, which gave us detailed instructions on how to do this. We were taught many things in boot camp that would prepare us for sea duty. For example, the markings on the piping (these were black and white stripes) that would tell us what was in that pipe. Steam, water, fresh or salt, Air, and some times the purpose of the element in that pipe. We also learned many nautical terms, rope knots, bugle calls, fire extinguishers, and how to stand watches. I remember my first watch. I had the twelve to four A.M. I stood guard at the main entrance to the administration building, at the front door. I fell a sleep, just for a second, I remember snapping to attention, then I worried for days afterward that somebody may have come by and seen me.

We were taught navy regulations and discipline. The penalties for disobedience, and personal hygiene. We were physically perfect, my teeth were perfect, except for one filling. We learned how to row a boat. Eight or ten men would sit in the boat with oars up. Then on command we would row in unison, and maneuver according to our coxswains command. We spent time on the rifle range, and had to get a score of marksman before we could graduate. We also learned close order drill with a rifle, and how to clean it. I loved the swimming pool best of all. I could swim the length of the pool back and forth several times without stopping.

The food was great as far as I was concerned. I remember one supper. I loved the blueberry pudding, and had several helpings. On the third or fourth trip to get some more, I found a cock roach in my pudding. That ended my wonderful supper. Generally the food was good, and I had no complaints.

There was one thing that impressed me more than anything, I can remember about boot camp. On the main road leading down to the administration building. They had two large six by six foot pieces of iron that were six and eight inches thick, with a shell hole in the middle of it. The conclusion being, that if we were to engage another ship with six inch guns. It would have six inch armor plate protecting the main parts of that ship. The same with the eight inch or what ever size gun the ship had for its main battery. The U.S.S. Oklahoma had fourteen inch guns, with fourteen inch armor plate. The Japanese battle ship Yammamoto had seventeen point five inch guns and armor plate. To engage these ships in combat, the theory was to match them by gun size if possible. During world war two that didn't always work out that way. Boot camp lasted three months, and then we had our graduation parade and inspection. That parade field was about four foot ball fields long, and twice as wide. With all the one hundred men companies we filled the whole field. As I remember it, my company was right up front and a little to the left of center. We were very excited, as we had just short sheeted our chief petty officer, in the barracks. We hoped to get away with it, but he caught us, and we all had a good laugh. He was an o.k. guy. I was given a week's leave, then assigned to the battleship U.S.S. Oklahoma BB 37.

We left the Great Lakes Naval Training station, by the Great Northern Railroad. We traveled by Pullman coach, and ate in the dining car. It was the most elegant train ride I ever experienced in my life. We passed through Minneapolis, Minn., and then a little further on we crossed the bridge over Elk River. I recognized my old camp site. As a thirteen year old, I used to go camping their, with nothing more than a can of beans and a loaf of bread. I had to hide a tear as we went by, it brought back so many happy memories, and I felt that it would be the last time I would ever see that place again. I had always wondered where that train went, now I would find out. The train was pulled by a big steam engine, and we were having a great time looking out of the windows. There were about ten or twelve of us on this draft. We ate in the diner, with real linen table cloths, and real silver knives, forks, and spoons. The colored porters were very polite to us, and treated us with respect. It was wonderful to sit at the dining table and look out the window at the country side, while the porters served us breakfast. We wished this would last for ever. As we sat at the table, we wondered what was in store for us in the years to come. Six years is a long time to a nineteen year old kid, who had just come out of the north woods of Minnesota. We passed through North Dakota, and into Montana. I remember looking out the window, at the yellow stone river, and seeing a lot of big fish in the river. (I could see clear to the bottom of the river) I made up my mind that I would fish that river someday. I remember the vast open expanse of the prairies of Montana, and the huge copper mine in Boise, Montana (I think). Then we were in the rocky mountains, and into Idaho. The scenery was beautiful. The train stopped for a while in Spokane, Washington. We got off the train to walk around. I saw a young Indian girl, about my age, selling apples. (The big Delicious kind.) I thought she was nice so I bought an apple from her. We soon were on our way, and it was late when we arrived in Seattle. We left the train and was soon on a boat that took us to the Bremerton Naval ship yard, where the U.S.S. Oklahoma was finishing her yard overhaul. The "Okie" was an old battle ship, being commissioned in 1917. I remember the stair treads. They were a quarter inch thick and about an inch and a half wide, strips that were wound like a spring, welded with spacers to hold the strips a part, and formed like a parallelogram, that formed a stair tread. The many feet passing over them, over the years, had worn them half way through. This always amazed me, "I would think." Imagine the number of times this ladder was used.

I did well on my mechanical aptitude tests, some of the guys had to go to school before going to sea. I was lucky and made it into the engineers, (we called it the Black Gang). I was assigned to the "A" Division, or the auxiliaries.

The ship was clammy and cold, as her boilers were shut down for over haul. My first breakfast on board was with the second division, and the mess captain was a first class gunners mate, with a very loud voice, but a nice guy. After breakfast he told me I was assigned to the "A" Division, and he would have one of his sailors take me around the ship, and show me where my steaming stations would be. I remember standing near the officer of the deck's watch station, while this sailor was getting his orders. I kept hearing these sounds near me. They seemed to be coming from an open hatch, or ventilation duct near me. Finally I called down, and asked, who's there, and where are you? A voice came back, and said, they were in the machine shop. I didn't pay any more attention to that, and went with this sailor around the ship. I learned the 'A" Division was made up of the auxiliaries, (Ice Machines, Evaporators, Dynamos, (D.C. Current), Steam Steering, Air Compressors, and the boat shop, (Boat Engineers). My first job was compartment cleaner, from there I went to the boat gang. I was assigned to number three motor launch. We usually served about three months at a job, then went some where else. We also had our turn at Mess cook. We had our mess tables in the same vicinity as our bunks. Some of the Battle ship crews still slept in hammocks. Our quarters were on the main deck amid ships, on the starboard side of the ship. That's just about at the water line, maybe a little above by about a foot. I had two mess tables to serve with around twenty men. If we were good and fast, and was able to serve our meals with out having the food get cold, we would get a tip at the end of our two weeks tour of mess cooking. There was a lot of competition, as every body was after food at the same time. Our main interest was, to study our rating manuals. Mine was the fireman second class, and first class, and another manual on Diesel engines. The Blue Jackets Manual was also studied and practiced. I stood my first cold Iron watch in the dynamo room, it was cold and damp. I had no idea what those machines were, and what they did. It had never occurred to me, where electricity came from. Our yard over haul was over around the end of August 1940. We got underway around five o'clock in the morning. I remember waking up, to the sound of our collision alarm. Looking out the nearest port hole, I saw a railroad freight car, and a tank car floating by. We were in collision with a barge hauling railroad cars across the Puget Sound. As we continued along Puget Sound on our way out to the open ocean, there were some whales on our starboard side. It was a beautiful day, with a brisk north west wind, and a bright sunny sky. When we reached the open ocean, we turned south towards Long Beach, California. My underway watches were in the main engine room. I was the J.V. phone talker. I wore a set of sound powered earphones, and communicated with the fire rooms and the bridge. For example, the number one or up to number four fire room, would request permission to blow tubes. I would pass the request on to the engineering officer in the engine room, and then on to the officer on the bridge for permission. The term, blow tubes, means that each boiler has a long perforated tube inserted between the boiler tubes. As combustion takes place in the fire box, soot collects on these tubes. The long perforated tube would be rotated as steam is released. Thus cleaning the outer surface of the boiler tubes. The soot is blown up and out of the ships smoke stack. This was done after sun set, so as not to reveal our position to any unfriendly ships at sea. My watch in the engine room was very scary for me. I had never seen an engine so large. We had a four cylinder triple expansion reciprocating steam engine. Our steam pressure was 300 lb. saturated steam. The high pressure cylinder was eighteen inches in diameter, the intermediate cylinder was thirty six inches in diameter, and the two low pressure cylinders were six feet in diameter. The engine was about two levels high. I remember seeing the engine forward and reverse being controlled by two big levers on the side of the engine. Looking in to the crank case, I think I could almost stand up inside of the engine. The Oklahoma had two of these engines, in separate engine rooms. They were very quiet, and ran smoothly. In long

Beach I started my new job as a boat engineer. It was very interesting, and I loved to run the diesel engine in the boat, and get away from the ship. We had an early morning run ashore for supplies. I can remember the strong smell of oil from the oil wells in the area.

I had a friend, his name was Leo Kenniger. We used to study our fireman manuals together. We went ashore in Long Beach one Saturday afternoon. I remember going into the theater and looking around for a seat up front. All of the seats were taken, that was anywhere near the stage. They were taken up mostly by old gray haired gents. So we went up into the balcony, which was way off limits. Their were two little cupolas that were just beyond the balcony. We could reach them only by climbing over the rail, on the balcony and then on to the cupola rail and into the seats their. The girl on the stage, that was in the act of stripping, stopped her dance and waited for us to get settled, then she hollered up to us, and asked us if it was all right if she continued on with her performance. We said sure go ahead. We thought it was great fun, but the ushers came up and ushered us out of the theater. Next we went down to some bar room. Leo asked me if I still had that ten dollar bill in my pocket. I said, "Yes". He said give it to me, I'll pay you back when I get back to the ship. We had been trying to pick up some girls, and nobody would give us a tumble. He slapped the money on the table, and hollered out. Hey girls who's going to help me spend my money? The first thing we knew, two girls sat down at our table. They were older than we were. We bought them a drink, then left to go out for dinner. The girls took us to a Chinese restaurant. After we finished eating and we were leaving, one of these girls stole one of the restaurant's tea kettles. We went to the girls home. There were other sailors and their girl friends there too. We stayed all night, I slept on the couch setting up. The other sailors and their girls slept on the floor. That evening they tried to get me to drink a coffee brandy. Coffee with brandy in it. I didn't like it, and I didn't drink it. The next morning, we were in the kitchen getting breakfast, when there was a commotion at the front door. The girl that I was supposed to be with was setting on my lap. Somebody said a medical corpsman just came in. The girl on my lap, said OH! my gosh, my husband, and jumped up to see him. Leo and I went out the back door in a hurry. We thought we had a terrific liberty. Now we were seasoned salt's. We stayed in Long Beach for a week or two, then upped anchor, and steamed for the Hawaiian Islands. Arriving around the first of October 1940.

I think I made fireman 2/c at this time. That meant I would get a raise in pay. I was getting $21.00 a month, now I would be getting $36.00 a month. Also I would be adding a stripe on the wrist of my uniform. I had a red stripe around the arm pits of my jumper, on the left arm. The deck ratings had their stripes and rating badges on the right arm. That indicated I was in the so called black gang, (engineers). This white stripe on the cuff of my jumper indicated my rank. Two stripes, meant I was a second class fireman.

We didn't go into Pearl Harbor at first. There wasn't room for us. The quays built along battleship row were not finished yet. We anchored off Honolulu, in the open sea. As a boat engineer, when I was called to man my boat, I would go out on the boat boom, then wait for an ocean swell, or wave to come along, to lift the boat up to the boat boom. Then I would jump aboard. It wasn't unusual to have ten to fifteen foot swells out there. After a while we entered Pearl Harbor, and tied up to the quays, in what would be known as battleship row. Our tie up was at the spot where the U.S.S. Arizona is today. I was in #3 motor launch. A 30 foot open boat with a Buda Diesel engine. We had a crew of three. The Coxswain, Boat engineer, and bow hook, (seaman). The Coxswain would communicate his intentions to me by a system of dings on a bell. For example, one ding ahead, two dings, neutral, three dings reverse, and four dings full throttle, in what ever direction we were in. Of course we had to use a lot of common sense as to how much throttle we should use. The problem came when the Coxswain would come up to a gangway too fast, and expect the engineer to race his engine in reverse for all it had, to stop the boats from ramming the gangway. We traveled the harbor on many different missions, taking on supplies, from a supply ship anchored in the harbor. During this exercise, we would accidentally drop a case of oranges, then help ourselves. They were the big thick skinned ones, and delicious. The ice machine crew would always end up with some good cheese, apples, luncheon meats, etc.

I loved these days, we had plenty of good food. My favorite past time was coffee time. We went down to the ships service, and bought a big glass of milk, and two home made donuts. That was the best milk I ever had. Some mornings we went over to a place called Aiea landing. It was nothing but a deserted house, with a dock out front. It was very peaceful over there. In the early morning hours, we could lay out there in the sun, and enjoy every minute. Just to get away from the threat of war, and ship discipline. It was very relaxing. Later when the war started, I found out, that the navy had a secret radio station in that house. One of our guys got into a gun fight with some Jap spies, who were trying to get hold of that radio station.

Every so often, we would have, what was known in the fleet as the ready ship. That meant we had to be ready to get underway within a very short time. The ready ship had to keep one or two boilers on line and her engines ready to go. (The U.S.S. Nevada was the ready ship on the morning of Dec. 7 1941, and that was why she could get underway so quickly). We also had to carry a lot of guard mail. Which was mail from ship to ship, and also sailors that were arrested by the shore patrol. We took them to their respective ships. Our last trip took place at mid night. Some of these guys were so drunk, I would have to carry them up the gang way and then dump them on deck like a sack of grain. One time we took a sailor out to the heavy cruiser U.S.S. Raleigh. He was turning himself in A.W.O.L. (absent without leave). I guess the ships officers had too much trouble with this sailor. They refused to accept him, and we had to take him back to the shore patrol head quarters. The shore patrol then escorted the man to the main gate and told him to go, as he was now out of the U.S. Navy. That same night we made several trips from Mary's point landing, down past the ship yard, out to battleship row next to Ford Island, around the lower end of Ford Island by the heavy cruisers, past the Hospital ship Solace down past the Destroyer nest tied up next to the U.S.S. Whitney. To deliver some sailor to one of these destroyers.

We went almost up to Pearl City. On our way we passed a channel marker buoy, within twenty feet several times. Not knowing that, as we passed, our wake caused that buoy to bob up and down rather wildly, as we were going by at full speed. We didn't find out until the next morning, that a Coxswain, (I believe from a motor whale boat) had lost his footing and had fallen over board. There was an alert put out for him, but nobody had given us any idea where to look for him. He was clinging to that buoy Every time we went by, he would holler his head off at us, only for us to whiz on by, and wash him off into the water. He was very mad at us. On one of these trips we pulled along side of the U.S.S. Astoria, a heavy cruiser, and delivered a sailor with a guard mail bag. As he went up the gang way, I observed, what I thought was a very sharp looking group of sailors, around the officers of the deck station. These heavy eight inch gun cruisers with their long sharp clipper bows, looked awful impressive to me. I would liked to have requested a transfer from the U.S.S. Oklahoma, but was afraid to. I never really thought the U.S.S. Oklahoma BB29 was the safest ship to be on. I wasn't the only one to think this way either. After the war started these cruisers carried the brunt of the war effort in the South Pacific during the battles of the Coral Sea and Savo Island with the night actions. I was glad I wasn't on them.

In March of 1941, my younger brother Harry joined me on board the U.S.S. Oklahoma. He was only seventeen, having enlisted on what we called the kids cruise, which was an enlistment of three years. He was assigned to the Evaporators, making fresh water. It was common in those days for brothers to be together. There were several pairs of brothers in the "A" division. There were three Barber brothers that were close friends to me. They unfortunately lost there lives on Dec. 7 1941.

Going ashore now presented a problem. Harry was under age, (18 years old) and he wanted to be accepted with the guys, and he wanted to drink also. I wasn't very good to him, but I felt responsible for his well being on board ship. It was against the law for him to drink alcohol. I had promised my mother I would look after him. Anyway Harry didn't appreciate it at all, when I revealed his age to the bar tenders. So he left me and went ashore with some other guys. Honolulu, in those days was a booming rough town, and not a very good place for young sailors. I was no exception either. On my first liberty ashore, I met up with a friend, that I had grown up with in Minneapolis. We used to deliver newspapers together. He was on the U.S.S. Boise, a light cruiser. (His name was William Orvil August Plate.) Bill wanted to show me Honolulu. He had enlisted about nine months before I did, and had been in Hawaiian waters for some time. We bought a pint of Four Roses whiskey, and we exchanged a swig of the stuff at our first opportunity. Neither one of us, was used to drinking , and we were drinking this raw, right out of the bottle. It didn't go over very well. It burned my throat and stomach. I said, "I don't want any more of that stuff". (We threw the bottle away.) So Bill Said, "I know of a place to go, lets try it". We went down Alaa street to a place called "The Pink Elephant". It was a Japanese bar, and they served "Saki", a rice wine. The instructions were to drink it slow. Well , I drank it slow, but not slow enough. The drink was very mild, almost like a sweet syrup. I began to feel very strong, and was going to break up some chairs, so Bill started me back towards town. As we went down the street, there were these signs for the local businesses, and they hung down quite low, because the Japs were a short people. I had to duck my head every time I passed under a sign. After a while I got tired of ducking, and I took a swing at them. This caused some commotion, to the point that Bill had to get me sobered up. We went into a "Sawmin" joint. Which was nothing more than a vacant spot between two buildings. There was a picnic table and a small Japanese cook who made this soup, and when he set his bowl of soup in front of us, I noticed two or three or more, of what looked like cock-a-roaches. They could fly. They came out of a crack between the bricks, up high. They flew in a circle and came down towards my soup. I noticed the Jap. had a dirty swab, that he used to clean the grease off the top of his stove. I grabbed the swab and swung it around my head at the flying cock-a-roaches, and managed to wrap it around that Jap's head and face. Of course he had to yell, and scream bloody murder, and run out into the street. Bill grabbed my arm and we ran down the street, back to where we came from, with a dozen shore patrol, with whistles blowing, in full pursuit. We ran down Alaa street, then ducked between two buildings, and out of sight. We waited until about 11:30, before we came out, and caught the last bus back to Pearl Harbor, and the last boat back to the ship.

The next liberty ashore, I went with a friend from the ship. We didn't have any plans. We were just going to explore Honolulu. I remember going by a tree that had flowers growing from every branch. It was beautiful, and the aroma was that of a flower garden. There was a statue there, of some king (King Kameamea, I think that's how you spell it) of the Hawaiian people. The story on the statue, said this king ate 49 dozen birds egg's for breakfast. By the size of the statue, and the king's belly, I believed it. We came to this hotel, and we went in, I don't remember why. There was a kind of waiting room, and it smelled sweaty. We sat down. Then this women came in and called to her girls. These girls were older than we were, and not very attractive. Each girl picked a sailor and sat down next to them. The one that sat down next to me, started to unbutton one of my thirteen buttons on the front of my pants. I told her to keep her fingers to her self. I was getting very embarrassed. I got up and told my friend, I am getting out of here, you coming? I left. Somebody in the room started to give me a hard time. Until I looked at him. I was ready for a fight. I didn't go ashore with anybody after that for a long time. It wasn't much fun going ashore alone. One day, I decided to go back down Alaa street again. I wanted to see where we had ducked out of sight, that night the shore patrol was chasing us. I went by this place called the Red Front Cafe. There was a Lucky Strike advertisement in the window. I went in and sat at the bar, and ordered a beer. Everybody sold beer those days. I never saw an ice cream stand in Honolulu. I never really liked beer, it was a beverage you had to get used to The place had a juke box, with an intercom connected to a record library in Honolulu. I soon found out that I could call in and play any record I wanted.

By this time I was getting very home sick for the north country, and the pine forests, and everything I had left behind in the C.C.C. camp. I was getting any where from $3.00 to $7.00 every two weeks, for my pay. It wasn't much, but I managed to save up $10.00 for a book on birds of North America. That helped some, but I missed the smells of the northern pine forests. With this place I could play records like the Indian Love Call, from the movie Rose Marie. Also the Donkey Serenade. I brought these songs to this place, and met this Japanese girl. Her name was May Yozackie. (The spelling of Yozackie is a guess) May had a talent for knowing how to handle home sick service men. I think she knew thousands of sailors, what ship they were on, where they came from, and there main topic of conversation. Some were married and had children at home. Me, I talked of the northern Minnesota forests. We had a little game going. Each time I came in there, I would have a song, she didn't know, and she would have a song for me. I introduced, the William Tell Overture, 4th part, theme from the Lone Ranger. She gave me Maui Chimes, A song that I have been hunting for ever since. I went so far as to send for my picture album from home. I took it out to May, and showed her the pictures of my days in the C.C.C. camp, and the story of my pet deer, and the three legged deer. We sat upstairs in her apartment, as I related these stories to her. I almost gave in to temptation, but wouldn't because I would not violate my values. When it came to mixing the races. I never had any idea how old May was. I thought she could have been in her thirties. It was hard to guess the orientals age, it seemed to me they looked very young until they reached their forties, then they seemed to age over night. I left the album with her that night as it was too late to try to send it home. I planned to send it home on my next liberty a week later, Sunday Dec. 7 1941. In the morning we got under way for fleet exercises, and "Darken ship at sea." I guess I had been going out to the Red Front Cafe for most of 1941. Bob Kinderman, Harry, Mike, and the Barber brothers, had all been there with me. We liked the place, it was better than the Honkey Tonks down town. It was Bob who managed to get her picture.

The picture I have in this book. We gained the confidence of these people. One time we went there, and she invited us to sit at the special table, behind the bar. We had just returned from a trip to San Francisco, California. During this trip we encountered a very bad storm. We lost a man over board, when we were trying to put up some batten boards around our 5" broad side guns. This sailor went over board and then he was washed aboard the U.S.S. Arizona, and landed on her quarter deck. Thinking he had washed aboard his own ship he tried to get to his locker for some dry clothes. Only to find out, that he was on another ship. He was lucky. In those days when two or more battleships traveled together, they formed a single line, one behind the other. During this storm, the seas, and waves were so big, that our propellers would come out of the water. This would cause the engines to speed up, and when the ship settled back down in the water, it put a tremendous strain on the drive shafts. We broke the starboard shaft, and cracked the port shaft. We changed our course from San Diego, North to San Francisco.

We spent the month of September anchored out in the harbor, within a short distance from Alcatraz, the Federal prison. I had the third watch, and that meant I had to wait for three days before I got liberty. It was just as well, because I learned that "Frisco" was a bad place. Two thirds of the first and second watches that went ashore came back to the ship with a venereal disease. My first liberty, I went with Mike and Bob Kinderman. We went roller skating. We were very happy and devilish. We were having a good time. I met a girl, and didn't know she was only sixteen. She told me she was in high school, I thought she was too young for me. We skated around the rink. She invited me out to meet her parents, and have Sunday dinner with them. That was O.K., I hadn't had a home cooked dinner in almost two years. We were to write to each other, when we left to go back to Pearl Harbor. Her name was Barbara, but I can't remember her last name. I do remember her address, it was 229 Chenery, San Francisco. We wrote once or twice then lost contact. Mostly because the war started and we didn't have time or materials to write with. San Francisco was a tough, wild place. I met a lot of seedy people there. How I tolerated them, I don't know. One liberty, I went across the bay to Oakland, and went roller skating. It was a Wednesday evening and girls night. I didn't know that, until I was in the rink. Most of the girls were college students. I was the only boy there and a sailor to boot. The girls came on too strong for me. I got out of there as fast as I could.

Back in Pearl, we went out to the Red Front Cafe, and we were given special treatment. We sat at the table in back of the bar. (The family table.) We met more of May's family, and during our conversation, they mentioned our stay in San Francisco. When we heard that we clammed up, and didn't say anything about what had happened on our trip to the states.

Liberty now was more strained than ever. There were street fights, and we heard of a soldier stabbing another soldier.

I was going ashore with Bob Kinderman and the Barber brothers, and Mike. I went with these guys because they were decent. No swearing. We usually had one drink, then a movie, or we visited every whore house in town. Just to talk to an American girl, and see the new styles the girls were wearing. The armed forces were running these places now, and were recruiting these young girls from the states. Their was a navy doctor that examined these girls every day. Of the thousands of military personnel now in the Hawaiian area, venereal disease was held to a minimum. One sailor run into his sister in one of these places. That was quite a shock to him. The navy transferred him to the east coast, and sent the girl home. To say the least we were tiring of this routine. But we missed the girls back in the states.

We were feeling more tense than ever. We didn't have radar in those days, and never operated at sea without running lights. Now we started to operate with darken ship. Down in the engine room, we were testing our ability to operate the machinery with the lights out. We were allowed to have a flash light to read our gauges. On deck things weren't going to well, because two or three weeks before this trip we were in collision with the U.S.S. Arizona. Now this time the aircraft carrier U.S.S. Enterprise was coming right at us, and turned at the last second, and in doing so, the carriers bow came over our stern, and bent over our flag staff and the plane crane. In my situation, I didn't keep up with world events. I never entertained any thought, that we could be attacked. It was just an impossibility. Yet that night, my friends and I were standing on the quarter deck after dark. Trying to sight the other ships in our group. It was pitch black out there. We could look down into the water and see a fluorescent glow where the ships propellers were churning the water. We could also see a fluorescent glow along the side of the hull. Just before the carrier came close enough for us to see her, the hair seemed to stand up on the back of my neck, and we became terribly frightened.

We thought something was out there watching us, probably a Jap submarine. We were discussing this when the collision alarm sounded, and the carrier's bow loomed high over our head's.

We entered Pearl Harbor on Friday afternoon Dec. 5, 1941. I had liberty, so I went right out to the Red Front Cafe and picked up my picture album. Then went over to the Army and Navy Y.M.C.A. to package it, to send home.... When I arrived, the place was jam packed with U.S. Marines. I met a friend from my C.C.C. camp. His name was Dwight Spurgeon. He seemed very frightened. I felt sorry for him as I knew the Marines had tough treatment. I believe they had just arrived from the states. I waited a while, but couldn't get near the desk. I decided to wait until Sunday when my next liberty would come up, then ship my album home.

During these days of 1940 and 1941, we were constantly training for possible emergencies, that could occur, during a surface engagement with an enemy ship. We would practice shell hits in a certain part of the ship, and we would simulate fighting fire and shoring up a bulk head with 2 x 4's and mattresses to keep the water out. We also had gas mask drills, and treating the wounded. Our experience with air planes, consisted of our spotter plane. They would tow a sleeve target over head and our five inch anti-aircraft guns would fire at it. We also had four, fifty caliber machine guns way up on our main mast. We didn't have very good anti aircraft protection and we knew it. We figured our ability to out maneuver the enemy ships, gave us our advantage. Because our engines could go from full speed ahead to full speed astern almost immediately. Our top speed was only about 18 knots. I don't think any of us realized the deadly effect of the air plane in delivering a bomb or torpedo.

We believed our blisters (another metal skin built on the side of the ship about two feet out, and covering the area of the armor belt), would protect us from serious damage.

When the aircraft carriers came into port. They always launched there aircraft. The planes came in over the fleet, and made dive bombing attacks at us. Then they would land on Ford Island. This was a defensive maneuver, as the planes could not take off from the carrier, until the ship was under way, and going at full speed. They could take off from the ground.

When we entered port this time, instead of tying up where we used to tie up, (the place where the U.S.S. Arizona tied up that day), we were placed just out board of the U.S.S. Maryland. We were at the head of the line. I was really concerned, I thought we were being set up for something. The scuttle butt (information) being circulated around. We were going to have some movie people come aboard Sunday, and take pictures of us. I was still uneasy, we were sticking out there like a sore thumb. I thought it was funny, there were no aircraft carriers in port. Our anti aircraft ammunition ready boxes were locked up, and the firing pins on our anti aircraft guns were removed. I didn't know this until the day after the attack.

A year earlier, we took on board a draft of about a hundred sailors. No word was given as to where they were going. We got underway and on my birthday (Dec. 19, 1940). A day or two later, we launched my motor launch #3, and we made three trips to a waiting cruiser some distance away. It was the U.S.S. Houston. Which was based in Manila, in the Philippine Islands. We delivered the last boat load, and when we turned around to come back to the ship. The ship was gone, we could see it disappearing over the horizon. We couldn't figure that out. Then the Heavy cruiser U.S.S. Houston got underway and soon disappeared over the horizon also. We thought the ship had forgotten us. We made a calculation as to our position in relation to Hawaii, and set a course in that direction. We steamed all day, and was almost out of fuel, when the ship showed up on the horizon. They took us aboard about nine o'clock that evening. In the process of lifting the boat out of the water I was trying to get that big hook in to our ring a swell came by and raised the boat causing my hand to rest on the exhaust pipe and burned my finger. I didn't get anything for supper, and as it was my birthday, I was supposed to get a birthday cake that evening. The guys told me they ate it.

The location of the refrigeration, (We called it the ice machines) plant. Is important in this discussion. The engineering spaces were located between the No. 2 turret and the No. 3 turret. There were four fire rooms, two abreast just aft of No. 2 turret. Then came the other two fire rooms aft of them. Next came the auxiliaries. On the port side, were the ice machines, in the center was the Dynamo's, and the evaporators on the starboard side. The port and starboard engine rooms came last in separate rooms. This being the very heart of the ship. The fourteen inch armor plate extended from the No. 1 turret back to the No. 4 turret, with a six inch thick armor deck. We were told we were indestructible. Our guns could sink anything that challenged us. The big "E" painted on our turrets testified to there accuracy. I had a hard time trying to figure out. Why an all steel ship could float anyway. Especially when it had a fourteen inch thick steel belt around it. It was a very scary time for me. With the size of the main engines, and when the main battery fired during target practice. It made the ship roll side ways, and the noise was horrendous. Coupled with the complete obedience to my commanding officer. I was going around in a sort of bad dream. Everything was so strange, and I longed for the safety of the northern forests.

Saturday, Dec. 6, 1941, I had the duty. My watches were from 4 PM to 8 PM, and 4 AM to 8 AM Dec. 7, 1941, in the ice machines. As I was looking forward to making the 8 AM liberty boat ashore, my relief, Mike Galajdik, relieved me fifteen minutes early. I took my clothes off and placed them in my locker, (my locker was located in the Ice Machine room). Wrapped a towel around me and with my shoes on, a bar of soap in my hand, I headed for the engineers showers, (head) on the main deck starboard side of the ship. That meant, going up three decks to the main deck.

My brother Harry arrived at the same time, coming from the evaporators. We were just about to enter the shower, when the general alarm went off. Our first reaction was consternation Why would the officers call general quarters on a Sunday morning? Last month, we had a change of command. The new Captain came from the Philippine Islands, and we didn't know him that well. Later we learned he wasn't on the ship. Naturally we began to blame him for the general quarters. That meant no liberty that day. May Yozackie was going to take me out to the royal Hawaiian forest reserve today. I had been working on that all summer and fall. Suddenly, the officer of the deck came on the intercom, "All hands man your battle stations, God Dammit, get going this is it". Just then, "Boom" the ship seemed to dip forward a little, actually the bow came up. I grabbed my shoes, and towel, and ran for my battle station, Repair #5, in the machine shop. Located just aft of the ice machines, and just over the port and starboard engine rooms. Arriving there, my job was to close the armor hatch to the main deck, when the station was fully manned. Mean while, I sat down and put my shoes on. Then I tried to borrow a pair of pants from one of the guy's, who had his locker there. He told me to go get my own. I was disappointed to say the least. I was totally naked, and had to face the possibility of fire, and all kinds of unforeseen difficulties, and I was afraid, also there were a lot of sailors going by on there way to battle stations. Then we were hit by another torpedo. It must have hit near us, as the ship seemed to leap up about a foot and a half, or maybe just the deck under me. The noise was horrendous. There were two explosions. I can recall seven torpedo hits in all. Years later, I learned we were hit by nine torpedo's. Some of these hits were simultaneous. With the second hit, my feet were knocked out from under me, and I landed on the deck. At this time I was really getting excited, my mind seemed to be whizzing so bad, I thought it was going to explode. I wanted to cry, but I had to control it. I didn't want anybody to know I was such a coward. The lights went out, they seemed to come back on again. Then another torpedo hit and they went out for good. All of this was taking place at once. I thought I was going to die at any moment. (The following are thoughts, I didn't have time to say them out loud), "OUR FATHER WHO ART IN HEAVEN, HALLOWED BE THY NAME", BOOM, BOOM, my thoughts were scattered I tried to say the LORDS prayer again, but couldn't. I thought I'd try the TWENTY THIRD PSALM. THE LORD IS MY SHEPHERD I SHALL NOT WANT, HE LEADETH ME, BOOM, BOOM, I felt like I didn't have time to say a prayer. In desperation, I said, "LORD I PLACE MY LIFE IN YOUR HANDS". I calmed down immediately. I found I could see in the dark. I could make out forms around me. I could think, and that terrible buzzing sound in my head was gone.

The officer in charge, a Mr. McCullough, Lieutenant, as I remember, wanted that armor hatch closed, as the battle stations were manned. I went up the ladder with another sailor to close the hatch. We couldn't budge it, the ship had too much of a list to port, and the hatch was hinged on the port side. This hatch was about four feet square, and six inches thick. On the edge it was stepped down two inches at a time. When this hatch was set during normal times, it took us about an hour to pry it loose, as during the years the hole in the deck became warped. To tell the truth, we really didn't want to close that hatch. Orders were orders, and tried everything, pry bars, brute strength, we gave up, and came back down to the machine shop. We realized that here was a hole where a bomb could go through, it added to our fears. Then one of our crew said, "This is enough for me, I am getting out of here." The officer in charge said, "Somebody stop that man." I was in his direct line of escape, I directed him into a large vertical drill press that I was hanging on to. He hit his head and went down. I felt sorry for him, as he had done exactly what I wanted to do, but didn't have the courage to. We then had a call on our J.V. phones. The evaporators wanted help to remove the bonnets on the sea water intake valves. The evaporators were on the starboard side, and flooding the starboard side of the ship, would help prevent the ship from capsizing. Mr McCullough was standing right in front of me, and my friend Bob Kinderman. It was logical for him to point us out to go. My legs began to feel like rubber. I didn't want to go down there for any reason. I knew it was too late to go down there. I could see that greasy stinking pump room under the evaporators. It made me sick even in normal times. Then two first class machinist mates volunteered. I was afraid the officer wouldn't let them go, as they were too valuable, but he did. They were very brave men.

Later that day, when the ship had capsized, sounds were heard from within the hull of the ship, tapping sounds. An effort was made to rescue these men. A burning torch was brought aboard and they were almost through to these two men, when the cork and oil caught fire, and these two men were suffocated. These thoughts have bothered me for many years, as I was so close to them. I was afraid the officer wasn't going to give the abandon ship order, and we were doomed to die right there. I was beginning to shudder at the thought of being submerged in that filthy black sea water with all that raw sewage in it. When the officer asked the man on the J.V. phones (Sam Smith) if he had heard anything about abandon ship. Smith answered in the affirmative. The officer then gave the order to abandon ship. I was the first one up the ladder, as I had just come down from there. I tried to open that water tight door, that had been dogged down. It wouldn't open. I called down for help. Five or six of us braced against the opposite wall. The door gave a little and water began to come in from all sides. I shouted, "stop were under water". Everybody started down the ladder dejected. I said to my friend Bob Kinderman, "what about that ventilation duck over head"? I remembered my first day on board ship, could this be the same opening on deck? I am taller than you. Get on my shoulders and I'll help you up. He said, "No you go". With out a second thought, I was up on his shoulders, and with my arms up over my head, I started up. It was then, I had second thoughts. Would there be any obstructions in this shaft, would there be any sharp edges left by the cutting torch, when the work men removed, what was in there at one time. Would there be cross members, that were usually installed to keep the shaft square. What would be at the top of this shaft? Would the hatch cover be open? How would I open it? I was still naked, and once I started up, there was no turning back. I couldn't back up. I was fully stretched out. I couldn't pull my arms down around me, there wasn't room. I could just move my fingers and my toes. Would the hatch cover be open on deck? I hadn't seen it open since we were in the ship yard, back in Bremerton, Washington. It had been by chance, that a sailor was showing me around the ship. I had heard voices coming from that hatch. We were standing near the Officer of the deck's station, when I heard those voices. I had called down, and asked where they were coming from, and discovered they came from the machine shop. Now would I be coming out at the same place. Being new on the ship, and there were so many things to learn, I soon forgot all about it. Now suddenly it was the only way out. Panic started to grip me. I made up my mind that as long as I looked upwards in to the eye's of "GOD", I could persevere. I knew that when I reached top and that hatch cover wasn't open, I couldn't back down to the machine shop, as there wouldn't be enough time, before the ship rolled over. Besides, I would be upside down. It was like being in a straight jacket. When I got to the top, the hatch was open. I looked out for what seemed like a long time, slowly my eye's focused, and I made out the white teak wood deck, with water coming up towards me. I scrambled out. I have never been able to figure out how I did that. I some how was able to turn around so that I could bend my legs at my knee's and slide down to the deck. Then call down to the men below, "Come on up, the hatch is open".

I hunted for over thirty five years, to find out who opened that hatch. Then one Dec. 7, I had just finished a speech at our local Kiwanis club, and stopped at my brother Harry's house. As usual we talked about that day. He suddenly said, "Didn't I tell you". What I asked? Remember when we met in San Francisco in 1944 at Treasure Island. You had just come back from the So. Pacific, and were on your way to Maine on a thirty day leave. I was waiting for orders for further assignment. Well, one evening I met MM1/c Slagter in a bar room, in San Francisco. You have a picture of us. We were discussing how you escaped. He said that he was going by that hatch that morning and a thought came to him. That he should open that hatch as somebody may want to escape through there. It should be noted here. This man had over fourteen years in the U.S. Navy, and he knows full well the consequences were to break water tight integrity. A general court martial, with years in jail or in time of war, death. We were under air attack, and at general quarters. Yet he set all of that aside and opened that hatch. I feel in my heart that GOD acted upon him. Also he had been on that ship a long time and he must have known about this as a possible escape route.

I stayed there and helped the guys out. My friend Bob Kinderman came out and reminded me, we should seek cover, as we were under air attack. We were trained to seek cover. I started to leave, but noticed everything seemed to stop, so I went back, and continued to pull the rest of these guys out. When the last man came out, I hollered down. "Is anybody left down there?" The assistant engineering officer answered. "He said he was to large to squeeze through that small opening."

I replied, "I would go hunt for a rope and pull him up. He said, "don't bother, it won't work". I went to find a rope, and went into the living quarters. This was at the break in the deck, from the main deck aft. A Chief Master at arms was there with a drawn pistol in his hand. Telling us to stay under cover, as we were under air attack. I sat there for a moment, I remembered that poor officer down in the machine shop. I said I am going to look for a rope to pull him out, and I left there. I noticed I wasn't the only sailor there that was naked. I kind of expected to be shot, and was relieved when I got outside. I went into the boat shop, but didn't find a rope. As I was looking, I came upon a locker full of clothes. I took a pair of pants, and was going to put them on, when I thought better of it. I reasoned if I was caught with another man's clothing, I could be court marshaled for steeling. If I was killed, they might bury me, thinking I was that man. We didn't have dog tags at that time, (actually I made my own dog tag when I went aboard the USS Massachusetts.) I put the pants back, knowing I had to face the fire and oil in the harbor. The ship lurched to port, and I found I couldn't get back to the door way. The ship was going over. I jumped up to the overhead track that led to the door. Hand over hand I made it to the door. I slipped my leg around the bulk head, and got up and ran as fast as I could up and into the water, with the ship coming down on top of me. I dove right into the super structure, and oblivion.

Going back to the beginning, when Harry and I were about to take a shower, and the first torpedo hit. Harry left for his battle station. He went down to the evaporators. Upon arriving there, the Chief Machinist in charge, told Harry that was no place for him. Harry was a kid of eighteen years. The chief in that station sent him up to repair eight. Which was way up forward, in the bow, and in the living quarters. Unknown to me, he passed right by me in the machine shop to get to the main deck. As he ran along the passage way, on the starboard side, through the engineers living quarters, the second torpedo hit, and he recalls the whoosh of dust and air rushing towards him, from the port side. He reached repair eight, and in a very short time the ship started to roll over. He ran in the dark, for the ladder and escape hatch. He made what I describe as the mad dash. Scrambling up the ladder, the hatch had been dogged down, but in the middle of the hatch, was an escape hatch. Which you turned a wheel, and the dogs, holding it down, pulled in and you could push the cover up and open. As he scrambled up through, the ship rolled over. Hands were grabbing at his legs, and he had to kick them loose, to get up through. How he got into the five inch broad side gun case mate, he doesn't know. They found themselves in the ship upside down and in a small air pocket. There were four of them. After awhile, Harry thought he would try to escape, as the air was getting stale in there. They were standing up to there necks in water. He ducked down under water and began to swim out ward, feeling along the ceiling as that was the bottom now. He bumped into the breach of the broad side five inch gun. From that he determined where he was. He followed the gun barrel outward. He swam into the hawsers that had broken when the ship rolled over. It scared him, and he returned to the air pocket. He bumped into the legs of the guys, and they reached down and pulled him up by his hair. They discussed what he had experienced. Finally two of these guys decided they would try their luck. They went, and didn't come back. Harry stayed awhile, then told this other guy that he was going to try his luck again. The other guy was crying. This time Harry was able to push the lines to one side and slid through, and headed for the surface. His lungs were bursting when he reached the surface. When he opened his eye's he couldn't see, as they were covered with oil. After blinking several times, his eye lids cleared. The oiler Neosho (Navy oil tanker, filled with gasoline) was in the turning basin near him. He started to swim over to the ship. Some body threw him a life ring and missed. He was swimming over to it, when a motor whale boat, from the U.S.S. Oklahoma picked him up. An old friend pulled him into the boat and said, "Look who we got here". It was J.D. Neil F2/c, one of Harry's friends.

They took him to Ford Island. He wasn't feeling very good so he decided to lay down. When some body placed a large piece of canvas over him. He laid there for about a minute when he got up and went inside the nearby building when a 500 lb. armor piercing bomb landed right on top of that piece of canvas. A chief petty officer came by and rounded everybody up and sent then by boat over to the sub base where they signed up with the rest of the Oklahoma sailors. Then hunted me up. He found me on the docks unloading wounded sailors from the boats and carrying them up to waiting ambulances. We spent the rest of the day together, as we knew we would be assigned to different ships from then on.

Harry stayed on the Island and helped form the Pearl Harbor Patrol. After two years, he was transferred to a diesel school in the states, and was later assigned to a Y.T.L. (A yard tug boat) and sent out to Saipan in the Mariannas.

When I came up, after the ship rolled over on top of me, I was out in the harbor about a fifty feet from the capsized battleship. I was stunned, I just couldn't accept what was going on around me. A plane coming from Mary's point landing was coming towards me. I was aware, that he was shooting at me, but I wasn't trying to get away. Suddenly, the bullets swept right by me, to my left, splashing water in my face. As the plane went by, I noticed the pilot looking at me, so I waved back to him. He didn't answer, so I waved again. This time he waved back, I thought, what am I waving at him for? I should be shaking my fist at him, and changed my out stretched hand to a fist. But he was gone. I watched as a dive bomber dropped a bomb on #2 turret of the U.S.S. West Virginia, and saw several sailors fall to the deck. It was the bomb that killed the captain of that ship. I noticed three life rafts, one on top of the other, that had floated to the surface. I climbed on aboard. There were other guy's climbing aboard also. We soon were splitting these life rafts a part to make room for more sailors. A clutch of life jackets appeared next and we were throwing life jackets to sailors in the water. I threw one to a sailor, and it landed short. This sailor didn't seem to make any effort to reach for the life jacket, so I jumped in the water to take it to this sailor, who seemed almost lifeless. I got about ten feet, when the fumes from the oil took effect, I was in trouble. I turned to go back to the life raft, but couldn't, as I was loosing consciousness fast. I looked beyond the life raft about a hundred feet away, and saw a boat going at right angles to me. I raised my arm and the coxswain in that boat saw me, and changed his course straight towards me, and pulled me into the boat. To me it seemed like a miracle, as I didn't have the strength to go another foot. I was completely done in. My head was pounding, and I was throwing up black oil, I was completely covered with oil. There was a roaring fire not far away, and I was sick. We soon filled the boat, and started across the bay. A plane came over us, but the coxswain managed to dodge the bullets. We landed near, what we called the mine docks, only just a little further beyond, as we landed on a dock that was filled with Captains, and admirals barges, (Boats). A marine with a rifle came up to us, and said not to touch any of those boats with our greasy hands. I went up to him, and pushed his rifle aside, and told him, "Come on Mac— there's a war going on out there, we need help picking sailors out of the water". Then I went by him.

I started down the road towards the Submarine base. As I went along, a sailor rushed up to me, and put a life jacket around my middle, and pointed to a house and porch where some woman and children were standing. A plane came down and strafed the road we were on. We had to scramble to the sides of the road. The other sailors started to scream and yell ouch. To my amazement, they were stepping on cactus leaves with bare feet. They had clothes on, but I was naked, and I still had my shoes on. I was covered with oil. I wanted to get some clothes, and wash the oil from my body. Some of these guy's manned those boats. A panel truck came, and picked us up, and took us to the Submarine base. I went to the showers. With bright work polish and carbon tetrachloride and salt water soap. I managed to get most of the oil off. I was there when the U.S.S. Arizona blew up. That sound, I'll never forget. It made me feel sick to my stomach. It seemed to be a dull hollow thud, but with great magnitude. Everybody stopped what they were doing. We all knew something terrible had happened. The base personal opened up their "lucky bag". I found a pair of pants and a shirt, and shoes. I went up to the roof, and tried to get one of the sailors up there to let me take a shot at a plane as they were coming over. No body would give up their rifle, so I went looking for something I could do to help. I found my self down on the docks helping unload the wounded from the boats, that were coming in from the harbor. Then load these people in to an ambulance. I talked to every coxswain, and boat crew to look for my brother, Harry. I was there all day and the next day. Around three o'clock that after noon, a sailor lifted my hat from my head. I knew it was Harry, and leaped a cement wall about five or six feet high, and instead of hugging him, we set to slugging each other on the arms, as if we were fighting. That

Louis R. Mathieson
Petty Officer 2/C

U.S.S. Oklahoma BB37
Shows #3 Motor Launch

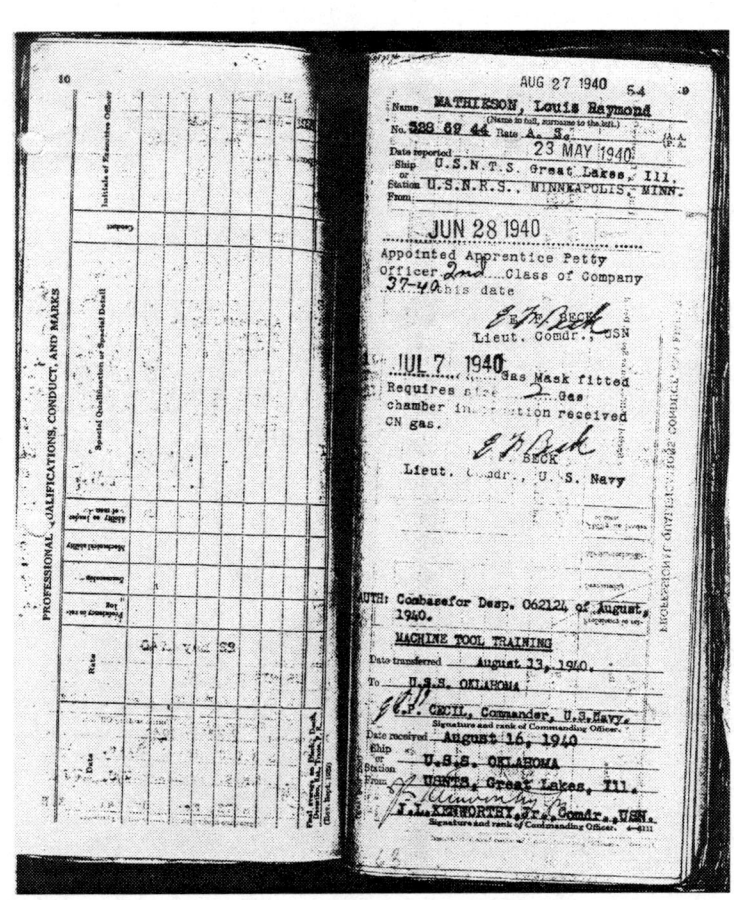

USS Oklahoma 1940

Harry Mathieson and A.G. Slagter MM1/C.
*This sailor opened the hatch that made it possible
for me to escape from my battle station
Repair 5 (the Machine Shop).
It was here in a bar in San Francisco two years later
that Harry learned this.*

Malcolm, Leroy, and
Randolph Barber.
*Three borhters who lost their lives
December 7, 1941.*

Capena Falls

Our private swimming hole. Louie, Randolph, ??? Leroy Barber, Harry, ??? Mike.

Harry and I are the only survivors of the Pearl Harbor attack here.

The Red Front Cafe
May Yosakie

The US Cafe Honolulu
??? Mike Gladick, ??? Bob Kinderman, ???

was the end of my helping on the docks. I spent the rest of the day with him. We knew we would be separated now, and we didn't know where we would end up. We went down to a building and registered with the rest of our shipmates.

That night at two o'clock in the morning, I was awakened from my sleep. I was under the porch of the Sub. base barracks, laying on the dirt. I figured if we were bombed again, I would be safe, at least, until I could wake up enough to seek shelter. With four other sailors, we went aboard the U.S.S. Hull DD 350, A Destroyer.

We immediately went to work loading supplies, until around 4 AM, we finished, and then I was told to help fuel ship. At around seven A.M. we had breakfast. After breakfast we were called to quarters on the main deck. I was assigned to the main boiler room for the eight to twelve watch. That meant I had to get down there right away, and learn my duties.

We were getting underway at eight o'clock. This was my first watch in a fire room, and I had the job of attending fourteen oil burners. The burners were like a gun with a long barrel, that stuck into the front of the boiler fire box. The fire room was pressurized. That means, we had a steam driven blower, that was installed on the main deck, in a protected place, just aft of the living spaces. This blower supplied air to the boiler, and it was just over my head as I stood in front of the fire box. It supplied enough air to keep the fire room several pounds above atmospheric pressure. We had 400 lb. steam pressure and super heated steam at eight hundred and seventy five degree's Fahrenheit. I was expected to maintain that steam pressure by cutting in more, or less burners as needed. It takes a little practice and a feel to do this. I was having trouble getting acquainted, it was so new to me, and I was tired and scared. Things were going too fast for me. Besides all of this, the fuel pressure valve didn't work, and I had to adjust the fuel pressure manually by turning the shut off valve wheel. Every time I cut in a burner, I would have to adjust the fuel oil pressure, by this wheel. That seems easy enough, but the ship was maneuvering in the harbor, and

USS Arizona showing the fire which burned for days.

USS Maryland with the USS Oklahoma bottom beside her. In the rear the USS West Virginia still engulfed in fire. The USS Arizona is behind the West Virginia spewing black smoke.

USS West Virginia with the USS Tennessee in the rear. This picture shows the raging oil fire.

Capsized USS Oklahoma with the USS Maryland, showing the fire-scarred hull of both ships.

```
PTK42 18 GOVT=SN WASHINGTON DC   DEC 27 1941 1229P

MRS ELLA MATHIESON=
=474 EAST AVE HW=

=RE LETTER NAVY DEPARTMENT ADVISES =THAT LOUIS R MATHIESON
AND HARRY L MATHIESON =USS OKLAHOMA LISTED AMONG SURVIVORS=
THEODORE FRANCIS GREEN.
                                                  .107P.

R L.
```

USS West Virginia with the USS Tennessee beside her in the back. You can make out the two cranes on the stern. Each ship has a crane on the stern to lift the airplane out of the water.

I found my steam pressure gauge wavering up and down like a yo-yo. As we moved out of the harbor, we got a submarine contact. The first thing I knew we got full speed jingle on our enunciator. The sailor on the throttle in the engine room spun his throttle wide open, and the steam began to drop. The seamen on deck rolled off several depth charges, set for shallow water. This was new to me and I didn't react fast enough. Another fireman on my watch pitched in and helped me cut in burners. We weren't fast enough. Then, "Boom!" the depth charges went off. The hull of the ship bulged inward as the ship seemed to come out of the water. I thought the enemy was out

there waiting for us, and we had been hit again. Now we had only 3/8' steel plate separating us from the salt water. A steam line ruptured, and was filling the fire room with live steam. The crew abandoned the station. I knew that if I was anywhere near that ruptured steam line it could cut me in half. I didn't want to go anywhere because of that. I guess I went in to shock as I was fading in and out of consciousness. This time my hands were firmly gripped on the hot fuel line, that fed oil to the burners. I hung on to this oil line to keep from being thrown to the deck. The only thing that was keeping me alive was the forced draft blower directly over head. I seemed to come to, after awhile.

Although I knew the crew was trying to regulate the break in the steam line by manipulating the valves by remote valve wheels on deck. I was afraid they would shut off the steam to the forced draft blower. I said a prayer. After awhile they managed to reroute the steam, and the escaping steam subsided. The crew came back down to the fire room, and one of the firemen had to pry my hands loose from the hot fuel line. I was like a "zombie." He took me over to the work bench and I sat there for the rest of the watch. I remember looking at my hands, expecting them to be blistered and half cooked. The temperature of the fuel oil in that line was around 150 Degrees.

When I got off watch, I went to look for a bunk to sleep in, and maybe some soap and a towel to wash up. I was told there wasn't any available. I would have to sleep on a mess table in the mess hall. All I had to my name was the clothes on my back, no tooth brush. During the attack on the U.S.S. Oklahoma. I was hit on the shin bone of my right leg. I had a big black and blue bruise, that had broken the skin a little. At the sub base I didn't go in for treatment, as there were so many there, that needed treatment more than I did. I went to the doctor on the ship, and he gave me sulfa drugs and a bandage. I needed rest, so asked for a blanket. Somebody gave me an old one. It was cream colored and faded. I went into the mess hall, and slept on a narrow bench, as the guy's were still eating. One of the worst memories I have of that ship was their so called, "Ice box bread". Bread, cooked ashore then stored in our ice box. Our tables had 3 inch edges on them to keep our dishes from falling to the deck in rough weather. A lot of my meals were had by dumping my food into a bowl, with my arm hooked around a stanchion, I ate with a spoon. My first meal aboard we had a good meal, meat, potato's, vegetables, and dessert. I ate a slice of that "Ice box" bread. It didn't take long, and I was on deck throwing up over the side of the ship. The guy's kidded me, a battle ship sailor, couldn't take a little sea on a Destroyer. It was no use trying to make any excuses.

We were on our way out, for the defense of Wake Island. We were escorting the Air Craft Carrier U.S.S. Lexington, along with two heavy cruiser's. One of the cruisers was the U.S.S. Portland, I have forgotten the name of the other one. There were five destroyers, the U.S.S. Hull DD350, U.S.S. Dewey DD 349, U.S.S. Monahan DD 351, I think. I can't remember the rest of them. I remember the Cruisers, with their long sharp clipper bow's. I thought they were so powerful. I thought they could sink anything that came our way. We cruised along side of the Carrier U.S.S. Lexington. She was the sister ship to the U.S.S. Saratoga. I would look up at those guy's on the carrier, and think that they were so safe. How wrong I was. The U.S.S. Lexington was one of the first ships we lost after Pearl Harbor.

My battle station was on No. 5 gun. A five inch anti-aircraft gun mounted on the stern of the ship. I was inside of the after deck house, where the ammunition hoist was located. My job was to take the projectiles from the ammunition hoist and hand them to a sailor on the gun it self. After awhile I was sent into the powder magazine. The powder magazine was located just below the after deck house, and under the gun mount. The two drive shafts went through the powder magazine. As luck would have it, we had our first air attack on my first general quarters in the powder magazine. I didn't have time to get acquainted with my station. The room was small and packed with ammunition. The gun started to fire, Brr-rang! The ship went to flank speed, and those two drive shafts created a sound like two sirens. The noise was deafening. I was so scared, tears filled my eye's, as I frantically reached for projectiles. I got them mixed up, and sent them everything, but anti-aircraft projectiles. Later I was told to memorize the locations of the various projectiles. I was having a terrible time adjusting to these conditions, but they were happening so fast, I couldn't cope with them. FEAR; It was so bad I couldn't eat. My stomach had a nerve that wrapped around it like a vise. Each morning we went to General Quarters one hour before sun rise and in the evening one hour before sun set. Being at war was a lot of work, we were working night and day. When we came in to port we worked all night and got underway the next day.

Coupled with my situation, no bunk in the living quarters, no clothes, my clothes now were filthy, I wasn't getting my rest, I was exhausted. My leg was also not getting any better and, it was beginning to swell. Ever since that first day when the depth charges went off, our fuel tanks were split, and they leaked oil, to the extent, we couldn't use them. We only had the middle tank which we called the sluice tank. We had to take on fuel every other day, from either a cruiser or the carrier. I was on the fueling detail every so often, and my clothes would get a soaking of fuel oil and sea water every time. For my part, fueling at sea consisted of holding the fuel hose, with a line on a hook attached to the ship, and trying to keep that hose in a sluice box. Invariably, the hose would be pulled out and between the sea's coming over the side of the ship, I would get a bath of sea water and fuel oil. Bunker "C" is a black thick sticky oil. Much like molasses. Where I had just gone through a bath in fuel oil at Pearl Harbor, it made me sick, and it also agitated the sore on my leg. The smell of the fuel oil also made me sick. Every day when I stood my watches in the fire room I got my hands into that fuel oil, also the smell was everywhere, it was so bad that it spoiled my appetite. I soon found that I could sleep much better if I slept in our motor whale boat out on deck. I used the life jackets for a pillow, and padding to lay on. The bad part came when the fire rooms blew the soot from their tubes at night. Some times it would rain, and I would wake up all wet.

We crossed the international date line on the eighteenth of Dec. 1941, the next day was Dec. 20, 1941. My birthday was Dec. 19 1941. I missed my birthday. For a long time I used to say, I had my birthday early that year. "Dec. 7, 1941, and my birthday present was my life. Now that I am older, I tell everybody that I'll never grow old, as I haven't had my twenty first birthday yet.

When we arrived at Wake Island, we were told that we were a day late. The Jap's were already there ahead of us. I thought we would go in and try to retake the Island, and rescue the surviving personal. I was looking forward to it as I had a friend (William Orvil August Plate Fl/c). who was off of the U.S.S. Boise a light cruiser. I would have liked to have been able to go in and rescue him, even though I was terribly frightened at the time. I never could figure out why the admiral didn't attack those Jap's on the Island That night the U.S.S. Hull was going to be a decoy. We were to break radio silence and imitate an air craft carrier, launching aircraft. We were to start broadcasting at mid night. We were to broadcast for an hour, then try to escape the best way we could. The odds were against us getting away. I knew we couldn't get far as we had only three days supply of fuel, and our steaming time to Pearl Harbor was over ten days away. At this time I was so exhausted, I felt if the ship went down, I could never survive long enough for another ship to come by and pick me up. At midnight, we got a message from Pearl Harbor to cancel all previous orders and return to base, as admiral Nimitz had taken command of all naval forces in the Pacific, and our orders were to return to base.

We arrived back in Pearl Harbor around the end of the year. The U.S.S. Hull DD 350 went into dry dock to have our fuel tanks welded tight. We took on supplies. I tried to get paid, but the pay master told me he didn't have time for that, I would have to wait. We were getting under way tomorrow morning. We stood our watches, and in our spare time, the gunnery officer would have us practicing loading shells in our loading machine. The Idea was to get that projectile and powder can into the breach of that gun as fast as possible. Our lives depended upon it. My leg was bothering me, and I knew it held me back. I tried, I felt I could never count on being alive from one day to the next.

I used to say a little prayer, when I tried to go to sleep at night. It went like this, "Now I lay me down to sleep, I pray the lord my soul to keep, If I should die before I wake, I pray the Lord my soul to take." The prayer helped me, and I would day dream about things that I would like to do some day. Up until now I had never given much thought about getting married. I hadn't met anybody that I really wanted to spend the rest of my life with. I couldn't recall anybody I'd ever met. Most guy's had pin up's of movie stars. I think that "God' must have entered my thoughts, as a thought came to me to pick out a picture of the girl I wanted. I picked a picture from a package of needles my mother had. I also dreamed of, some day leaving the navy, going across a large body of water to a little town on the shore, pick up this girl, get married, and come out of town, going up and over a hill, and building my home in a field over looking this body of water. I also wanted to cross the western part of the United States, much the same way the early settlers did. It was as if I was talking to GOD. I wanted to get a chance to regroup.

I couldn't cope with this situation as it was now. I was getting weaker every day. If the ship went down, I knew I wouldn't survive, as I was too weak. I also had a lot of compassion for the fliers on the U.S.S. Lexington. They would take off every morning, and be gone all day. We were always looking to see if they still had their bombs, when they returned from their mission. Every once in awhile one or two wouldn't make it to the carrier, and would crash into the ocean. One day we were the pick up destroyer, and we picked up a flier who, had just crashed into the ocean, he had both ankles broken. He tried to dance on deck and fell in a clump on deck in great pain.

One of my prayer's included these air men from the U.S.S. Lexington, also the B17 bomber crews over Europe. My thoughts were to some day, after the war was over, to have the names of these flier's placed across the screen in a movie theater. Which would signify the tremendous sacrifice, and effort these guy's were doing. Twenty six years later, I went to the movies to see, "Midway", I cried when I saw those flier's name flashed across the screen.

After a while I resigned myself to the idea that I would die. The hardest part to except, was that nobody would remember me. My mother would receive a telegram saying, "Missing in action". Looking back now my prayer's, must have really echoed across those Pacific skies. My leg began to swell, and my clothes were getting grubbier every day. You can't imagine how dirty the air over the ocean can get. With the blower over my head in the fire room. The dirt was accelerated. We came in to Pearl Harbor at the end of the year and I still hadn't been paid, nor given any clothes, and I still had to sleep on the mess table. We didn't have time, we worked all of the time loading supplies, repairing our engines and boilers etc. One time I had to go into the fire box on our boiler, to lay up some brick that had fallen down. I was picked. They had to lift me up and pour me head first into the fire box. The fire brick was still hot as it cooked my feet. I could stay in there for only a short time. I remember telling them not to light the burners until I got out of there. What a feeling it was to go into that combustion chamber. It was as if I was standing in front of a firing squad. Those fourteen burners looked like rifle barrels. I couldn't get out of the fire box with out help from the outside. I had to come out head first and somebody had to lift my body up until my feet came out. Coming out of the fire room we went up the ladder and through the air lock and then out flush with the deck.

The second time in, I received ten dollars from the navy relief fund. I spent some of it for a towel, tooth paste, tooth brush, soap, and a comb. I also received some mail, this time in. One letter was from my mother. She told me she was moving to Rhode Island, to be near her mother, sisters, and brother. She also wanted to know why Harry and I hadn't written to her. She didn't know whether we had survived the attack. The letter was sent to the U.S.S. Oklahoma. Years later I learned that she received a telegram from the war department on the 27th of Dec. stating that Harry and I had survived. We didn't have any stationary and never gave it a thought about writing her a letter, we didn't have time.

I sent Harry a guard mail message and the next day we got together and we went ashore and into Honolulu. I was able to borrow a suit of dress whites from one of my shipmates. We went down to see May at the Red Front Cafe. The place was Jam packed with sailors. There wasn't room to set down in the place. As we were leaving May saw us and hollered "Math-e-son", and she came running over, and grabbed me around my neck and kissed me. I was really taken back at this kind of reception. She was crying and wanted to know how many of my friends had survived the attack. I had to tell her about Mike, and the Barber brothers. As we talked I began to realize, what a wonderful person she was. That was the last time I saw her.

We got under way the next morning. I remember one night when I got off watch, (I had the eight to twelve watch) I was tired and went to sleep. The General alarm went off, and everybody went to their battle stations. We were told there were three Submarines under us. The carrier fleet had left us, and we were to sink them. After about fifteen minutes, we secured from our battle stations, and wait for morning. I slept through the whole thing.

At four AM. we again went to general quarters. As I came up from the mess hall, I looked out over the water. The sea was flat calm, and it had these strange things all over it. They looked like little half round sails, floating on the water. They were about two or three inches in diameter. I'd never seen these things before. The guys told me they called them "Spanish Men-O-War", but stranger then that, I had a dream that night, and they were a part of that dream. I began to feel apprehensive. I was wondering if to day was going to be my last one. The guys told me we had a pack of submarines under us. My leg was really giving me a hard time now, and I was late getting to my battle station in the powder magazine. Somebody took my place, and I was to help with the depth charges. These guys were the nicest guys I ever met. They helped me all the time. I borrowed everything from them, mostly cigarettes, and that can be a pain. I remember a Chief Electrician mate, (He was a U.S.S. Arizona survivor). He was like me, he wandered around in a daze.

It wasn't long and we were firing our "Y" guns, and rolling depth charges off the stern. A lot of debris came up including a red colored barrel, cork and oil. Maybe some other stuff also. Anyway it resembled the image I had in my dream. We continued on, and sometime later we fired again, this time we had the same conglomeration come up on the port side. I was beginning to get real excited, as these events were just like my dream, that I had last night. The next time we laid a depth charge pattern in my dream, the submarine surfaced and fired her torpedos at us, and it was coming up our stern. When that terrible explosion took place, and that black water came up, I was sure that the bow of that submarine came up out of the water. I was telling the man on the JV phones to call the bridge and get out of there.

The first thing I knew, two hospital corpsmen were on each side of me, trying to calm me down. I sat down and tried to tell them about my dream, but to no avail. Finally, after many more depth charge runs, we ran out of ammunition, around three o'clock that afternoon. We secured from general quarters. The Captain announced that sandwiches would be made for us, as soon as the cooks could make them.

Years later, I saw a National Geographic program on T.V. about the Truk Islands (Japanese Naval Base, during WW11) They used under water diver's to go aboard a sunken submarine. The sub. was over 300 feet long, and during the war, we made a surprise attack on this base, and the submarine sunk it self. The divers recovered the submarines log book. In the log book, the captain wrote about this battle with a destroyer, at the beginning of the war. We were told that our depth charges were landing right on this submarines deck and going off. I used to believe that we sunk three submarines that day. Many years later in 1995, I went out to Fredericksburg, Texas, to Admiral Nimitz Museum. The Museum had a two man Submarine on display. The sailors on this Submarine were called, "Twelve Day sailors". They were "Kamikaze", and they had twelve days from the day they left port until they were sent to a target. They had the best food and a free run of the ship.

My friend Bob Kinderman, and I were coming up the deck and had reached our torpedo tubes, about midships, when I said, "Look, Bob out there, isn't that a periscope?" We watched, and then we saw the tell tale sign of a torpedo coming at us. Bob saw it and said, "It's too late, Louie, it's been nice knowing you." And he shook my hand. We expected to be blown up about then. Nothing happened, it was gone. We looked over the side of the ship and theorized the torpedo had gone under the ship. Just then the general quarters alarm rang out again. The captain announced, we had an unidentified ship on the horizon coming at us. He said we were out of ammunition, but still had our torpedo's. So we were making a torpedo run on this war ship. He said we would probably be blown out of the water before we got within firing range. As we approached each other each ship was sending out recognition signals, and at the last minute, we recognized each other. It was the heavy cruiser U.S.S. Portland, and we were to escort her into Pearl Harbor.

Of the five sailors from the USS Oklahoma that were assigned to the USS Hull DD350, two were transferred. K. F. Browne MM1/C, and L. R. Mathieson F/C. That left P.P.Bestudick MM1/C, C.E.Kelly F1/C, and R.R. Kinderman F1/C. These sailors remained on board ship through most of the Pacific campaigns, until Dec. 18, 1944. There were three destroyers that were capsized during a very bad typhoon. They were literally blown over on their sides.

Nine years later it was September 5, 1951. Harry and I were having a cup of coffee about seven or eight in the evening. We were setting at the table right next to the kitchen window when a knock at the window drew our attention. I couldn't see through the window so went to the door. I was surprised, it was Bob Kinderman, my friend from the old days on the Oklahoma. It was at the start of the Korean War, and he had been called back into the US Navy, and was stationed at Newport, Rhode Island, We didn't write that much during the war and his story was far too long to write about. In all his years of writing to me, he seldom wrote more than two sentences. I invited him in and we started to have a cup of coffee, when he said wait until I tell you this story.

Bob, in his own words: It was Dec 18, 1944 he was in the central Pacific near the Philippine Islands. He said he got off watch at 8 AM that morning, in the main engine room. (His exit from the engine room came out flush with the deck.) He went aft to the living quarters (at the after deck house). He for some reason took a shower and put on clean clothes. By this time he was aware of the ship taking severe rolls. He went up to the after deck house and looked out the door and observed that the sea was getting very rough. Later that morning the ship started to roll way over beyond the 45-degree list, almost side to. At this time he started to measure the time it rolled way over and waited for the ship to come back up right. At this time it became evident to him that he needed a life jacket, which he had left in the engine room when he got off watch. He knew of some life jackets that were on the number five anti-aircraft gun just outside and to the rear of the after deck house. He measured his time and when the ship rolled over again he took a chance and went outside and got three life jackets in time to return inside of the after deck house. He kept one and tossed the other two to the waiting men also in the after deck house at this time. He was surprised that they didn't fight over them, as there were several men that were present

He waited and measured the time the ship rolled over and when that time exceeded those few minutes he figured that she wasn't going to come back when he opened the door and left the ship.

Outside he could see the ship lying on its side, the smoke stack was gone and men were all over the sea, some were being sucked into the opening where the smoke stack had been. He said that his first reaction was to swim away from the crowd of men. The crew was drowning like flies. He described how the wind would blow him off the tops of the waves and he would go tumbling down to the bottom of the swell. He called it like a whirling dervish. He would come up, from, down there half drowned, only to rise up to the top of the next wave and the process would repeat itself. He did this all day from about nine or ten o'clock in the morning all night and the next morning. When the sea seemed to calm down. He observed somebody swimming some distance away, so swam over to where they were. There were six crewmembers in this group. He couldn't remember their names. A little later that day a rolled-up collision mat floated by. They swam over and clung on to the sides of it. That afternoon as he remembered it a shark came by and bit the guy next to him and chewed off the calf of his leg. They then pushed him up on top of the net so he would be safe, but didn't think about applying a tourniquet around his leg, as they were too busy trying to hang onto that collision net. He bled to death some time after that. After this took place they removed the outer layer of rope and went inside and tied the rope back to the mat so as not to lose the protection. During that next day one of the guys went out of his mind. He said that he could see a gedunk stand (ice cream stand, navy lingo) and he jumped off the collision mat and a shark grabbed him and that's the last time they saw him. Bob was afraid he was going to lose his mind also. He thought that he could see a ham sandwich lying on the mat beside him and he reasoned that as long as he could rationalize that it was a mirage, he would leave it alone.

On the third day during the late afternoon he caught sight of a carrier task group in the distance. It was coming right towards them. He watched it come along, but as it got almost up to them it slowed down, then turned away.

Now he was afraid that the carrier group wouldn't come towards them and they would miss their chance of being rescued. Then he thought: hey, they were sending off the night cover planes and now they would be taking back on board the day cover planes. Sure enough, that's what happened. He watched the carrier turn and come towards them again. Now the carrier came right by them, he tried to shout to get their attention. His mouth was so dry and cracked by the seawater he couldn't make a sound. Then another destroyer came up by, but went on by without seeing them. Then he thought, there is one more chance, the pick-up destroyer would come by. He watched and they too went by, but this time a sailor was about to throw the evening garbage over board when the sailor pointed to them; then he knew he was about to be rescued. At first he tried to stand up on deck but his legs gave out and he landed in a crumpled position on deck. He was carried below and put in a bed. They were thirsty and wanted water. The medics gave them only sips and just enough to moisten their lips. After a while they managed to get more water and something to eat. They were taken back to San Francisco, where they were assigned shore duty for the rest of the war.

I have another story about the USS HULL DD350. This one goes back to when I was on this ship. When you first went on watch you could have a cup of coffee. This coffee was put on the burner at the start of the last watch and it would boil for four hours As you can imagine it was very strong, I would pour more canned cream into my coffee until I had diluted it to where I could sip it for the rest of my watch. Pouring all of that canned milk into my coffee, when I went on watch is about all the nourishment I received during my short time on this ship. To say the least, it was hot down there, (as I stood right in front of the boiler with its fourteen burners), with the constant whine, or should I say roar, of the forced draft blower overhead. As I remember the front of the boiler was very hot, but the forced draft air was usually very cold and could be very wet if we had any seas coming over the side. The wind from this blower was constantly flapping my pants against my bad leg and it would rub that little Band-aid off in a very short time.

I remember the first class water tender (The man in charge of the fire room). Stolie was his name as I remember him. He was very interested in what was going on up above. He had to see for himself, so he went up through the air lock and was standing there with just his head out of the escape hatch right on deck, and was watching the air attack, when a piece of shrapnel fell on his head, killing him instantly. Our theory was to put as much bursting anti-aircraft fire up as possible, thinking that the attacking aircraft would fly into the exploding shells to bring it down; also, it would deflect most of the planes to miss their mark.

When we arrived in Pearl Harbor this time, I was notified that I was being transferred to the U.S.S. Solace, the hospital ship, for amputation. The doctor told me, he thought gangrene had set in, as my lower leg was turning black. I left by motor whale boat.

Going aboard the U.S.S. Solace, I was led to a compartment full of bunks. The compartment was dark and not too clean. It looked to me like living quarters. I crawled into a bunk and went to sleep. It was around 10 AM. I wasn't there long, when somebody woke me up, and we went way down aft, to a very clean ward. The sailors here had operations for appendicitis, and other types of operations. I went to sleep.

One morning, when my doctor was making his rounds. Somebody was shaking me, "Wake up, the Doctor wants you to get up out of bed," I said, "but my leg, sir." He said "your leg is all right." I got up and walked around the bed. The Doctor said, "Do you recognize me?" "No I don't". "Sit down." Then he sat down beside me. When you came aboard here, you were scheduled for amputation at the knee. I happened to be going ashore that day, and noticed your service record on the O. D.'s desk. (Officer of the dock). Your records disclosed the nature of your injury. I had you transferred to my ward, where I could give you some personal treatment. Do you remember playing pool in my recreation room back home on Portland Ave. in Mpls. Now I remembered, and was amazed that he would remember a kid like me. That was about five or more years ago. I think of these events, that were taking place around me were part of GOD'S work. I know it sounds a little far fetched, but that's what happened. I have gone over these thoughts and events many times, trying to figure them out, as you will see as I go along.

He said to me you've been asleep here for the past week, now I want you to get up and help the nurse here. You can wash the dishes, deliver the food to bed patients, and what ever the nurse wants you to do. You stay up around the nurse's desk. I did just as the nurse asked of me. After a few days, the nurse said, "don't you go to the movies? "No

I don't care that much". She said, "Would you like to go with me tonight"? Well when we walked down the isle, down front, all the guy's whistled, and made cat calls. It suddenly dawned on me. We were going to sit down front with the officers. This nurse was a lieutenant. I thought she may have liked me, and I perked up. That went on for a few days, until one night, I was on deck, and saw her hugging and kissing another officer. I realized then that she was doing this to get me on the road to recovery. Up until now I didn't have much interest in anything. I believed I would never live to see the United States again.

The U.S.S. Lexington came in with my ship, the U.S.S. Hull DD 350. I went up to the doctors office. I requested transfer back to my ship. The doctor got really upset, and told me to go back to my ward. He would make the decision as to when I was well enough to leave the hospital ship. "But Sir, the ship will get underway tomorrow morning." He said, "Go". After the ship left the next morning, he let me go, and I found myself aboard the U.S.S. Whitney, the destroyer tender. I thought, I would have to be on board here for at least three or four weeks or longer, before my ship would come back in again. It also could take months before it could return again. I had to sleep on deck, as there wasn't room in the living quarters. My newly cleaned blanket was already streaked with dirt. It usually rained in Pearl Harbor every day or night. A couple of days went by, when my name was called over the speaker system, I thought I would be put on a working party, and I wasn't too anxious to report to the Chief Master at Arm's.

When I reported in, he told me I was being transferred. I thought, o'boy, here I go to another ship in the fleet. Then he said I was going to Boston, Massachusetts. It took a few minutes for that to sink in. I couldn't believe my ears. I really didn't think I would ever see the United States again alive. I started to cry, I didn't want anybody to see me cry, so I ran around the ship as fast as I could go. Until I could control myself. The chief finally caught up to me and told me to get my gear. The boat was waiting for me, He also told me I was assigned to the U.S.S. Massachusetts BB 59.

On the ship back to the states, I think it was the SS President Hayes a troop transport. The Boatswains mate in charge of the passengers, assigned us to working parties. My job was to chip paint and red lead the shaft alley. Now the shaft alley is a damp cold wet place, and dirty. I didn't relish the job, but would do it anyway as I would be there only one week. The Chief machinist mate in charge of the engine room, invited me to have a cup of coffee before I started work. In our conversation, he asked me what ship I had served on. I told him where I had been since the war had started. When I mentioned the U.S.S. Oklahoma, he told me he was an old "Okie" sailor. Then we talked the rest of the week about sailors he knew on the "Okie". He wanted to know who made it, and how.

We pulled into San Francisco, and got as far as the Golden Gate Bridge, then turned around and went back out to sea. I got really excited, as I figured something must have happened back in Pearl Harbor, and we were to go back out there. My chance to see the states was gone. Somebody was quick enough to see this, and assigned a sailor to watch over me. They thought I might jump over board.

We went to San Diego, California instead. We arrived the next day, and when we went ashore we were given liberty. I borrowed another sailors uniform. (He was an old guy, that had been in the navy during WW1. He had his WWI campaign ribbon on his jumper. When I went shore, the shore patrol stopped me and told me to cover up that ribbon, when I explained that I had borrowed the uniform, as I was a Pear Harbor Survivor.

I went to a dance at the local U.S.O. I remember the girls wouldn't dance with me when they saw the two white stripes on my cuff.

The next morning we were called to quarters, and I was given a choice; Ride by government transportation, (which was a fixed up cattle car, or by our own transportation, with 49 days delayed orders.) We were to report to pier 92, New York City, on May 1942. Everybody wanted Delayed Orders, except me. I didn't have any money, nor did I have anybody I could contact, to get me some money. The Navy hadn't paid me since Nov. 1941, and here it was the 24th of March 1942. I also didn't have a uniform. All I had was the clothes on my back, the same clothes I received the day of the attack, Dec. 7, 1941. I didn't have anybody at home I could call on except my Aunt Jennie, and I didn't expect her to help me.

The Officer, and the Chief Petty Officer convinced me to take the delayed orders. So I signed the papers. The Chief then took me down to the brig. (Jail) There we dug into a sailors sea bag, and took a dress uniform, shoes, hat, sweater, and "P" coat. Clothes from a sailor that was receiving a dishonorable discharge from the U.S. Navy. The uniform was filthy with puke and smelled like a brewery. I washed it and had to put the uniform on wet. I had to leave that receiving station by noon. I received $7.50 as ration money for the trip across country, had I traveled by train.

I sent a telegram to my Aunt Jenny in Minneapolis, and asked for some money, for that afternoon. I paid five dollars for the telegram and some cents. I know I had 2.35 left. I waited until the telegraph office closed at 5 PM. She didn't answer, so I started to hitch hike north to San Francisco that night. I didn't have a map, and I had no idea how I would get across the country except to head east, in the same manner the early explorers did by foot. I guess the first part of my prayer's were coming true. I think GOD was testing me now. I arrived in San Francisco the next morning, with a sore throat and a cold. I took a room in a hotel for 75 cents, and went to bed, with a chill. I slept all day till around 9 or 10 o'clock that evening. I got up and started down the street. I didn't get far, when an old friend recognized me from across the street. She was Mike Galajdik's girl friend. The guy that relieved my watch 15 minutes early on Dec. 7, 1941, and saved my life when he done it. She wanted to know all about Mike. I told her everything I knew, about him and the bad news. I had a hard time getting away from her. In the early hours of the A.M. there wasn't many rides, so I walked. Some where I met a Chief Petty officer fresh from Pier 92, New York City. He warned me to keep my nose clean. The commanding officer there had it in for enlisted men. Some sailor had his daughter pregnant. He told me every sailor going through that station would have his hair cut off. He showed me his bald head to prove it.

I passed through Sacramento, and then in the late afternoon I walked across the great divide. The sign post called it the "Donner Pass". I remember going around this big rock. It went from summer warmth to winter cold, and a snow bank as I rounded the corner into Nevada. My cold and sore throat was getting worse. I had to spend another 75 cents for a hotel room in Reno Nevada. The next day I felt better. I counted my money and had 75 cents left. I had spent 15 cents in San Francisco for a hamburger, before I left there.

My next ride would have to be all the way in to Salt Lake City, and that was 500 miles away. I spent all day on the out skirts of the town of Sparks, next to Reno, Nevada. That night a guy came along and offered me a ride. He said he was going out about a hundred miles to a Mine. He would let me off out there and I could hitch a ride both ways, until he would return to Reno. He said," come with me, at least you will be warm most of the night". I did. Around midnight he left me off, in that high country it was cold. I ran up and down that road to keep warm. I swung my arms, and shivered for two or more hours. Then he showed up and we went back to Sparks. I remember going into a diner across the highway and asking advice on how to get to Salt Lake City. They told me not to take a ride, unless it was all the way to Salt Lake City, as it was too dangerous out on those high plans this I time of year. I made Salt Lake City around five or six o'clock that afternoon.

I hadn't had anything to eat, since I left San Francisco, two days ago. Now I was hungry and I only had a few cents left in my pocket. I had to make a decision, what could I get to eat that would give me some energy right now. A hamburger? but that's too expensive. I chose a frappe. I went in a drug store, and I remember looking up the street and seeing the Mormon Tabernacle.

Back out on the road. A guy came along and said there was a better road East from Ogden, Utah. I went with him. When I got in Ogden, he left me off, and I had to go into a gas station, to ask for directions. I was told there was no road east, and I would have to go back to Salt Lake City. It was around eight o'clock when I started back. There wasn't any traffic that time at night in those days. I walked all night, and some time that next morning I arrived back in Salt Lake City. After two days and two nights, I was tired. It's about thirty five miles between those two towns. I don't remember much about that night. I must have walked in my sleep, sometimes I think of that poem, "Foot Steps in The Sands Of Time".

I stood on the road and hitched hiked a ride with a truck driver. I tried to stay awake to keep him company, but I couldn't. I would drop off to sleep, then wake up a while. I remember going by a small country school, with the students horses tied up out side.

Five miles out side of Rawlins, Wyoming, the truck ran out of gas the driver gave me a gas can, and asked me to walk back to a country store some fives miles away. I did that and spent my last 35 cents for some gas. We arrived in Rawlins just as it was getting dark. I stood on the highway next to a store, and across the street was a diner. I could smell the food and thought about going over there to get something to eat. Then I thought about my identification, and the possible trouble I could get into. Remembering what that officer in San Diego, said "Don't tell anybody anything about Pearl Harbor, or how the war was going in the Pacific. I told myself I would drop before I would bum a meal.

A bus drove up to the store, and let passengers off. The bus driver went into the store, so I moved up close to the door to get warm. The bus driver came out and told me to move on. I began to feel desperate, would I ever get to New York City this way? I remembered my prayer's from out in the far Pacific. I wondered how those Pioneer's felt a long time ago, when they were out there going to a strange land, and wild Indians, and they were going to live out here and feed themselves.

I was cold and tired. A car came by and agreed to take me to the next town. They said they were going East to the war factories, and didn't have much money to take me very far. There were three people in the car, two women and a man. I figure they were in their late thirties. This being my third night with out any sleep, setting in a warm car, I fell asleep almost immediately. When I woke up, it was mid morning, and we were in Nebraska, and I had drooled on my neckerchief. I was a little embarrassed, and said, "I guess I fell a sleep, I thought you were going to take me as far as Cheyenne, Wyoming". He said we couldn't wake you". I said, "I guess I had better tell you something about me." I told them everything about me except, the extent of the disaster at Pear Harbor. He said, "you must be hungry?"

They stopped at the next town and we had breakfast. My first meal, (Two eggs, home fries, bacon, toast, and coffee) in six day's. As I look back on those days, I don't recall any great hunger pains, my attitude was great. I felt so lucky, I enjoyed just looking at the country side, the green grass, and the tree's. It was probably the very best rehabilitation the navy could have given me. I didn't worry about time, and I had gone hungry before. I remember having a nerve that had wrapped around my stomach, it seemed to cut my stomach in half. I am sure it was caused by fear. At times I wished I could have had more money. It would have been so much easier. I thought, some day, I would like to make this trip in more comfort, with some money. Anyway it was just what I needed to get my thoughts together, and to start out fresh, when I got back into the navy.

Although the Indelible print of the surprise attack, and those three months on the U.S.S. Hull DD 350, would stay with me for the rest of my life. I remember some thoughts I had just before leaving the ship. It was like having an argument with GOD. I wanted to get out of the war zone, to get myself together, so that when I got back into it, I could do a better job. I was vaguely aware of this conversation.

We arrived in Omaha, Nebraska that afternoon. I remember walking across the bridge over the Missouri river. It was night time when I went through Iowa. I didn't have the faintest idea about what road to take, as they were all rural now. I rode with several high school kids. They were just riding around.

I used their advice as to which road I should take to go north to Minneapolis. Eventually a truck came by, and took me into Minneapolis very early in the morning. On familiar ground I walked to where my childhood friends lived. I was told they didn't live there anymore, but the people told me where they lived down the street. I knocked on there door at six o'clock in the morning. They were just getting up, so I had a few minutes before they went to work. My friend Leo Nystrom, (We had grown up together.) They gave me breakfast, and then they had to leave for work. Leo's mother, Signe called the newspaper people, and had a reporter come out that afternoon. He wrote a story about me, and the next day my picture was on the front page. Later that day, the shore patrol came by and took me down to the recruiting office in Minneapolis. As I went into that office, I very quickly searched every person seated at a desk for a glimmer of recognition. Somebody who might help me as I was in deep trouble.

The recruiting officer, a lieutenant, took me into his office, then asked for my service records. I handed him my one sheet of mimeographed paper with my orders on it. He asked for my I.D. card, "I said I don't have one. How about a dog tag? "No" Then I told him the clothes on my back belonged to a sailor that was dishonorably discharged from the naval service, and they did not have my name on them. He told me that he had no choice but to put me under armed guard and escort me to pier 92 New York City. I asked him to call the receiving station in San Diego for verification. No, he couldn't do that. I said, "you've got me over a barrel, Sir. If you send me to New York by armed guard, that Captain will give me a dishonorable discharge. I haven't done anything wrong. I'll make a deal with you. There is a man out there in your office, I have never seen him before, but I think his brother was on board ship with me. Last year, I happened to be standing near him at mail call. When he opened his letter, he showed me a picture of his brother in civilian clothes. Now I think he is in your office. If I can identify him, will you let me go? We went out to his office, and I went up to this sailor and said, "is your name Rollo?" To my amazement he said, "Yes, you must be Louie Mathieson. I got a letter from my brother, just the other day, and he said you might be coming this way. I don't remember seeing his brother, but I could have. How ever a few years ago I received the roster of survivors from the U.S.S. Oklahoma and his name wasn't on it. This has always been a nagging mystery to me.

I had to walked back to Leo's house. I asked the Lieutenant for a ride back and he said no. I have a name for him, and it isn't a very good one. The next day Leo's mother gave me a telephone number to call. It was my mother, she was staying at a friends house. This was a great surprise to me, and of course for her too. She told me she came out to Minneapolis as my brother was going into the navy the next day. We got together, and went out to Grove City where Everett lived on the Farm. We had a great get together with the Oval's and some of Everett's friends. I had to tell them a little bit about my experience.

Back in Minneapolis, Leo was getting up a party for me with his friends. I had met one of his girl friends and of course I fell for her. I thought she was going to be the girl I would marry. Leo warned me, she wasn't worth it. Mom broke that up anyway. My mother and I went out to my Aunt's house and got my US Savings bond, cashed it, and bought a buss ticket to Rhode Island.

That week end Leo arranged a blind date for me. We went to this girls house, and he introduced her to me. We were about to get acquainted, when her 12 or 14 year old son called out, "Mom, can I have some money for tonight?" I was shocked, how could Leo, my best friend arrange a date for me that was married. I was so immature, I never gave the girls feelings a second thought. I said, "I wouldn't go out with them," and went back to Leo's house. The next day I left with my mother for Rhode Island.

At this time in my life, I was looking for a girl I could marry. That was one of my prayer's, and I wondered who it would be. I wanted somebody that I could write to and pour my heart out to her, and I had to have a girl I could trust. One that never had sexual relations before.

When my delayed orders time was up, I went into New York City and pier 92. My first objective was to get paid. I stood in line all day, and never made it to the pay masters office. After the second day, my name was called over the intercom, to report to the pay masters office. I walked to the head of the line, and walked in to his office. My mother had called the Governor of Rhode Island and told him the navy hadn't paid me since Nov. 1941.

The Pay Master gave me one hundred dollars. Not having any money for such a long time, I was afraid to spend it. Going ashore now, in New York City, it made me uncomfortable. I was afraid to spend it, as I would spend it in a night club. I remembered that liberty in California and that girl's house. I sent it home to my mother, I had no use for it.

We put the U.S.S. Massachusetts into commission on May 10, 1942. I was still getting a considerable amount of money and I had been out all night, drinking and when I went on board I looked terrible. I was ashamed of myself, and made up my mind I wouldn't do that again. I was beginning to feel proud to be a member of that great ship. I was assigned to the "A" Division, and the after emergency Diesel Generator room. The ship was tied up at the South Boston Navy yard. Coming aboard this great ship, I felt like I was in the movies. At times I would look at my hands to see if I was real, even go so far as to pinch myself. It was so wonderful to be aboard such a beautiful large modern battle ship, and it was brand new. I spent all of my time, learning my way around the ship.

I remember trying to figure out the quickest route to abandon ship. There were three routes that I could use, only to realize, I would never make it. I was too far down in the bottom of the ship to ever escape. I remember talking with my Div. officer, Mr. Jackson, about what it would be like to go down with the ship. We surmised that when the ship sunk to great depths it would crunch in like a tin can. I made up my mind that for me to survive, I would do my best in my job to keep the ship afloat and the guns firing.

I started by reading the instruction books on the machinery, studying the blue prints, and tracing the air systems, and pipe lines through out the machinery spaces, and learned how the remote air valves worked.

There was one big problem. "Shinover MM2/c" he would come up to the Forward Diesel and spend all morning lecturing my gang. He covered all subjects. I had to stand and listen because he out rated me. He was senior to everybody he told me, he was forty five years old. I was a F1/c and not a petty officer, and only twenty one years old. The year and a half In the us Navy I hadn't been in charge of anything. He had his good points though, he started us studying the various blue prints and learning how the machinery operated.

About three months on board they put me in charge of the Forward Emergency Diesel, and the forward two pump rooms. This was the first time I had received that much responsibility, I really didn't know that much about being in charge. Because of that I gave up on shore liberty and stayed on board and chased down pipe lines. We had the air systems, (which included both the main battery and the secondary battery). The main battery had both 200 lb. air pressure for gas ejection, and 3000 lb. air pressure for recoil cushion. These systems were also tied together in such a way, that would allow the 3000 lb. to supply the 200 lb. air when there was a need for it. The 200 lb. air pressure was used entirely for gas ejection. When the guns were fired the gas ejection, blew the smoking debris, and gas clear of the gun.

We also had two pump rooms in the forward part of the ship. These pumps supplied the fire hydrants and flushing sea water through our toilets. Which were nothing more than a trough with toilet seats spaced along the top of the trough, and small partitions between the seats. The water then ran out into the ocean. In the case of fire we started up another pump, which would raise the water pressure for the fire hydrants. These pump rooms also had an intricate system of valve manifold's, and valves. These same valves all had air motors installed on the valve stem, with the air being controlled from the damage control station around the No. two turret barbet. There were tanks located around the ship, and in the bottom, They were used to keep the ship on an even keel. These valves controlled the water going in and out of them. The problem was, some of these valves were installed backwards, you could get water into them, but not out of them. Taking the time to trace these systems out, and finding these errors, caused the division officers to take notice of me, and I soon found myself in charge of the forward emergency diesel generator room. We had several chief petty officers, Machinist mates take over this station, but stayed only a short time, when they requested transfer out of there. Why, at that time I didn't know. I would soon find out. I loved the station. I found that I had to work with the main electrical distribution board, located just above me at the next level. I met an electrician there who gave me a book on the elements of electricity. I studied this book in my spare time. The book was a first year text book for electrical engineering students. I did most of the problems, except the calculus math problems, as I never had calculus in high school. At this time I also picked up a book, High Speed Diesel Engines. This was an excellent book on thermodynamics of the diesel engine. I studied it, and read it thirteen times. I took my exam for machinist mate 2/c, and received the rating the first of August 1942.

One of the things I really enjoyed when I first arrived aboard was the half hour or so after our noon meal. There was a sailor who loved to sing. He would get on top of the after ventilation duct, and sing such songs as the Beer Barrel Polka, Row Row Your Boat Gently Down the Stream, Blue Berry Hill, and many other popular songs of the day. We had such a great time and it took away the stress, and worry, of what's ahead, in these terrifying times. At least it was for me, as I knew what could happen, even if it was a great modern battleship. The crew was mostly reserve sailors, with a few regular navy battleship sailors mixed in. We were to train these new guy's in the ways of the navy. I must say it was an almost impossible job. Especially since, the senior petty officer was a reserve. He was an old truck driver from Detroit, Mich. and a rough tough one at that. He would get us all together in the forward diesel and lecture to us all morning. We didn't get anything done. He was about 45 years old. I could never figure him out. He would be my friend one minute, and the next he would be cutting me down. He would undermine my authority. I would give one of my men a job. Then when I was off to the pump rooms to check on the packing glands on the pumps. When he would come by, and tell my men to take it easy, and go up on deck and get some sun. I couldn't put these sailors on report, as the report would have to go through him. Yet when he had a problem with a compressor, or a pump, or a valve he would call on me. I felt that he couldn't handle the job alone. He needed me, like wise I needed him. I was young, only twenty one, and inexperienced. I could run this station, and I spent a lot of time learning my area of responsibility. I studied the blue prints on the air compressors thoroughly, and the emergency diesel generator engine. I liked being in charge. This was the first time in the navy that I had a job like this. I felt that I didn't have to answer to anybody, except of course to my Division officer. What I didn't realize, this was a chief petty officers responsibility.

At first, when I went ashore in Boston, every girl I met I fell in love with. I remember this girl I would meet in the Cave, (A night club). She would come in with an older woman and sit next to me. I had a Tom Collins cocktail, I made the drink last as long as I could, (as I knew I couldn't drink more than that one drink as I would get drunk.) until she had finished her drink. Then we would go out on the Boston common, and lay on the grass. She liked to kiss me, but I couldn't kiss her. I couldn't figure that out at all. After a couple times like this, I asked her for a date for Sunday morning, I would meet her on a certain corner. She didn't show up. I didn't go back to the Cave after that. I soon found out that the girls in Boston weren't interested in me. I was really disgusted. Then I met a girl from an Island out in Boston Harbor, called, "Spectacle Island" I brought another sailor from my gang with me, Rob Case, he met another girl out there and we had some good times together. The girls lived on this Island so we had to take them home, and some times we stayed out on the Island all night and came back to the ship the next morning. How ever after the second night out there the girls didn't wake us up for the trip back and we had to get the Island Police boat to take us back. We stayed in my girls house and the girls stayed in the other girls house with her parents, (They were light house keepers). The second night we stayed out there, they didn't wake us either, so we had to steal a row boat and row back to the ship. That was the end of that love affair. I did however, provide for Rob Case's court ship and wedding and honey moon, as he didn't have any money. I was getting my back pay at this time so I was always loaded, so to speak. A couple more experiences like this and I gave up on trying to find a girl I could write to when I went back out in the Pacific. Instead I concentrated on my duties aboard ship.

The ship would have to leave Boston harbor every two weeks, for security reasons. We would either go up to Portland, Maine or down the coast to Norfolk, Virginia. One time we went into Penobscot Bay and over the mile course. This would set the shaft revolutions necessary for calculating our speed. One time we were firing our guns at Seal Island, at the mouth of Penobscot Bay. I never knew I would build my house on Penobscot Bay, and live there the rest of my life. At the time, I was down below tending my air compressors, and was completely unaware of where we were.

As the summer wore on I lost interest in looking for a girl, and even stayed aboard. Then one Sunday morning, around the end of August 1942, I went ashore alone. I just wanted to get away from the ship by myself. We were near the end of our fitting out, and would soon be going to sea and probably the South Pacific. In Portland I took a bus out to Old Orchard Beach. I had made a liberty there earlier that spring, before things got so complicated in the forward diesel.

Old Orchard Beach was a summer colony, with carnival attractions. Sunday was quiet and the beach was deserted. I roamed around all morning just relaxing. It never occurred to me why I was out there. Around three or four o'clock that afternoon I headed up the street to the bus stop, a little ways out of town. I was a little early so went back down the street, and was looking in a store window. There were several groups of people, and three girls coming up the street. When these three girls got right behind me, a loud voice rang out in my head, "There she is".

I just about jumped right out of my shoes. There's the girl I'm going to marry. I didn't know what to do. I didn't even see her face. I don't know what she looks like. Something took hold of my body and I found myself running across the street, and up the street, then back across the street again. Then standing at an angle, I watch these three girls, who were talking a mile a minute and not noticing this sailor who they had just passed, now standing in front of them again. I thought I was crazy running up the street like I did, even now as I watched them, I knew the girl in the middle was mine. My heart was pounding, and I was shaking all over. I just stood there and watched them turn down a street and disappear. The bus came along, and I went back aboard ship. I thought, How am I going to meet her, what's her name, will the ship get under way tomorrow? I was heart sick with worry. Finally, I said to myself, what will be, will be. I told myself that I didn't love her and in a few days I would forget her. Then after the war I could always come back here and look for her.

The United States of America

Navy Department ✠ Bureau of Navigation

N. Nav. 84 (Sept., 1929)

Navy Training Course Certificate

Louis R. MATHIESON having completed the Navy Training Course

Machinist's Mate Second Class

with a mark of 3.00, is awarded this certificate this 7th Day of August, 19 42. Notation to this effect has been made in his service record.

Lieut. (jg) USNR. **U. S. Navy,** Division Officer.

E. M. THOMPSON, Commander **U. S. Navy,** Commanding U. S. S. MASSACHUSETTS

U. S. GOVERNMENT PRINTING OFFICE 4—7104

Three days later. I had liberty and had to ask some body to go with me, as I didn't want to make any mistakes. I knew I couldn't walk up to her and get acquainted. I had to get somebody I could trust without having the whole ship know about this. Paul and I had been boat engineers on the U.S.S. Oklahoma. I considered him a trusted friend. I asked Paul Gloor, to go ashore with me. I told him I saw a girl out at Old Orchard Beach that I wanted to meet, but that I wasn't sure I had the nerve to speak to her. He started to laugh, but he noticed I was serious, and I needed help.

We hung around the board walk all day, I was afraid she wasn't going to show up, and I was going to leave. Paul held me back, and at the last minute, there they were, still talking a mile a minute. Paul went up to them like he had known them all his life. He brought them over, and we got acquainted. Her name was Vera Payson, and she lived on Ingraham's Hill, Owl's Head, Maine. We talked, I was afraid she had a boy friend, so I was trying to make the most of every minute I had before he showed up. She was cuter and nicer than anybody I had ever met before, I wanted to grab her and hug and kiss her, but knew you didn't do that to somebody you just met. Sure enough a young soldier showed up and they left. I figured I'd stay with her two cousins and she would be back. As luck would have it, they showed up about a half hour later, and the soldier asked me to take his girl home as he had to take his friend back to the base as he was drunk.

The USS Massachusetts

That was great, we walked around some and then I took her to her place of employment. We stood under the street light and she put her arms around me, under my pea coat, and I kissed her, good night. I was hooked from then on. I was happy, to say the least there isn't words in my vocabulary to express my joy. I saw her once more before we got under way.

We were to join up with a convoy, and escort it across the Atlantic to invade North Africa at Casablanca. On the way over we encountered a bad storm. Around midnight, one of my men, discovered water dripping from a drain plug on the intake manifold of the diesel engine, that powered the emergency generator. I went over to the control panel and took the engine off standby. Then called the control engine room, and reported the problem.

All of the engineering officers, and "A" division officers were down investigating the problem. I was told to get my men together, and remove the cylinder heads, to get started right now, as the day after tomorrow we would be going into battle. Well I knew I could never take that engine apart and get it back together again in that short a time. I did the next best thing. I called the first class machinist mate in the after diesel, (Shinover) as I remember his name. Together we drained all of the water out of the intake and exhaust manifold's on the engine. Then we went up through the ship and drained all of the water out of the air silencer, and the exhaust muffler. The water seemed to be in the intake manifold. Next we opened the pressure relief valves on each cylinder head, then rolled the engine over, by using a crow bar and inserting it into the holes in the flywheel. The water in the cylinders squirted out all over the ceiling. Then with the pressure relief valves still open, we shut the fuel off, and then gave the engine a shot of air from the air starting system. Making sure all of the water was blown out of the engine. We started the engine up. I think we had the engine running by the time the chief engineer reached his cabin. This was the beginning of a period when the division officer called on me for everything that needed to be fixed.

The morning of the invasion started off at about 4 A.M. Everybody was nervous. The warrant officer in charge

A Publication of Friends of Battleship Massachusetts

VOL. 19 NO. 4 WINTER 1992 FALL RIVER, MA

50 Years Ago

Mamie Goes to War!

French Battleship Jean Bart fires against USS Massachusetts from her quay at Casablanca on the morning of November 8, 1942. The small freighter in the foreground, Sainte Jacqueline, was sunk by "overs" from Battleship Massachusetts.

of my station was giving me a hard time over a fire extinguisher, whether the handle should be tied down or left alone. I wanted to test out my air compressors, and the emergency diesel generator, and the steam bilge pump, to make sure everything was ready to go. I didn't get a chance. We were fired upon by the French battleship, Jean Bart. Her first salvo sent a projectile through our colors, attached to our smoke stack.

We started firing, and I was busy watching the air pressure on the 200 lb. gas ejection system. The starboard anti air craft guns were firing steady at enemy planes, and the main battery, the sixteen inch guns were firing as fast as the guns could be loaded. We were receiving four projectile explosions on both sides of the ship. My guy's and I were trying to distinguish between near misses and direct hits. We took a hit on

It was the largest amphibious operation in history up to that time. Hundreds of ships and aircraft and thousands of assault troops would cross enemy beaches along hundreds of miles on the northwest coast of Africa. Operation Torch, named for the torch held by the Statue of Liberty and symbolizing imminent freedom for those enslaved by the Axis, began on November 8, 1942, and Battleship Massachusetts was there.

Under the command of Captain Francis E. M. Whiting the powerful new battleship was the flagship of Operation Torch's Western Task Force under Admiral Giffen, flying his flag in Massachusetts. The crew was untested in combat but had trained hard, and on the morning of November 8 enjoyed – or tried to enjoy – a combat breakfast of steak, eggs and pancakes before they went to general quarters.

It was not known if the Vichy-controlled French warships and troops at Casablanca would resist, but resist they did. When Admiral Giffen gave the order to "Play Ball," Battleship Massachusetts was the lead batter, demolishing port facilities at Casablanca, putting a shore battery at the fort at El Hank out of action, and sinking two destroyers, two merchant ships, a floating drydock, and putting the battleship Jean Bart on the bottom of Casablanca Harbor in the first American-Axis battleship gun fight in World War II. (The second would occur one week later in the Solomon Islands.)

In spite of minor damage from two enemy projectile hits, an electrical failure aft resulting from gun recoil shock, and the loss of a Kingfisher spotting aircraft (but not the aircrew) to enemy fighters, Battleship Massachusetts and her gallant young crew acquitted themselves with distinction, returning to Boston bloodied but proud.

It was the first of the Battleship's 35 engagements. The coming battles in the vast Pacific Theater would be long and dangerous, but none would remain in the memory of the crew as would Casablanca.

our starboard side, which knocked out No. Ten gun mount. A two gun five inch anti air craft turret. The hit caused the 200 lb. gas ejection line to leak air, but not enough, for the automatic air shut off valve to work. I was loosing air pressure, and thought it was caused by the rapid firing of the main battery. Somebody told me about the air leak, on the No. Ten gun mount, so I called the No. Four engine room, and had a fireman go over and shut the air valve off. I don't recall getting permission from the damage control officer, to do this. But in the exchange of information, about what I was doing I explained that the gas ejection system was loosing air pressure so fast I didn't have time to request permission. Mean while the main battery was firing so rapidly, that the gun barrels were getting so hot that the gun crews were using gas ejection air to cool them off. Thus causing the 200 lb. air pressure to drop. When the pressure dropped below 100 lbs. I called Mr. Wentworth over and tried to explain, that if the air pressure went below 90 lb's. The automatic air valves would shut off the air to every gun. That to get them going again I would have to go to each

65

Top:
V ... Mail
Love letters from the South Pacific

Center:
Louis Mathieson
Taken from the quarter deck onboard USS Massachusetts, anchored in Efate, New Hebrides Islands. 1943

Bottom:
USS Massachusetts
*Taken in Portland, Maine, Casco Bay early 1942.
I am standing on the main deck amid ships.*

PEARL HARBOR SURVIVORS ASSOCIATION

PINE TREE CHAPTER

Maine State Chairman
Robert Presnell.

President
Richard C. McCrum

Roster of Members Attending 34th Anniversary
Meeting at U.S. Naval Air Station, Brunswick, ME.
December 7, 1975

NAME	UNIT	RESIDENCE	NO. GUESTS
Joseph A.A. Bergeron	Ft. Kamahamaha 15th Coast Artillery	Brunswick	3
J. Heleodore Brillant	USS Phoenix (CL-46)	Topsham	3
Carroll J. Casey	USS Phoenix (CL-46)	Mexico	1
Redlon J. Cope	Schofield Barracks 63 F.A. BN 24th Div.	Cumberland	1
H. Fred Fischer		So. China	1
William C. Hushing	USS Detroit (CL-8)	Bath	0
Hollis G. Knowlton		Waldoboro	1
Richard C. McCrum		Orono	1
H.L. McLean	USS Chandler	Ellsworth	1
Louis R. Mathieson	USS Oklahoma	Rockland	1
Edward J. Perry, Jr.	Schofield Barracks Co. C. 804th Eng.	Bath	1
Orin F. Perry	USS Pennsylvania	Cape Elizabeth	1
Robert Presnell	65th Eng. Battalion	Portland	4
Eric W. Russell	USS Detroit	So. Harpswell	1
Robert E. Sadler		Thomaston	1
Forrest Smith		Winterport	1
F.C. Soares, Jr.	CGC Roger B. Taney	Mt. Desert Is.	2
Harry E. Taggett		Limestone	0
Paul Verastek		Portland	1
Ralph B. Vigeant	Camp Mala kole	So. Harpswell	0
Raymond Q. Williston	Schofield Barracks Co. A. 19th Inf.	Portland	1

Guests. Captain Richard S. Zeisel, U.S. Navy, Chief of S
Commander Patrol Wings, U.S. Atlantic Fleet, and
Mrs. Zeisel.

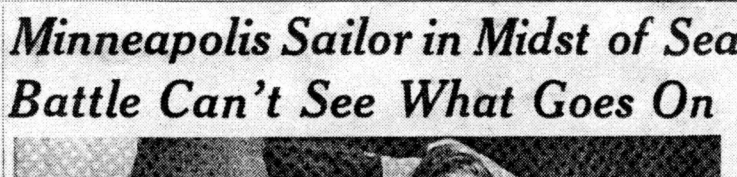

Minneapolis Sailor in Midst of Sea Battle Can't See What Goes On

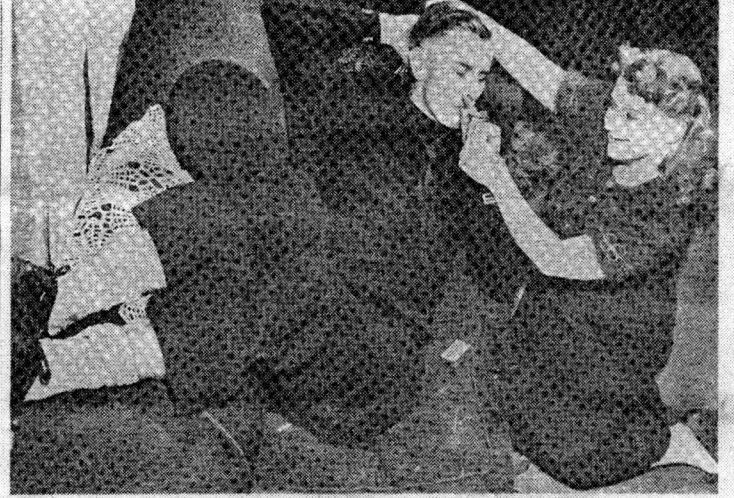

—Daily Times photo by Bob Paul.

FIREMAN, FIRST CLASS, LOUIS R. MATHIESON
Gets a light from Mrs. Lillian Haley, former schoolmate, as he takes it easy after duty in Pacific

Vera – June 1945
That beautiful morning we flew to New York City and then by train to Maine on our first three-week vacation. We lived here, 2810 Wentworth Street, Cleveland, Ohio.

Thelma Diporie, Louis and Vera Mathieson, Bill and Harriet ???

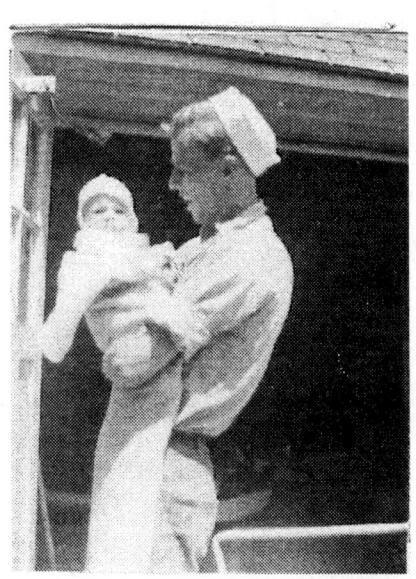

Johnny and Louie
Spring 1945
Cleveland, Ohio

John at 4 months

May 1946, just discharged from the U.S. Navy

valve and reset each air valve to each turret. I asked him to call the damage control officer, and have him slow down on the use of so much air. I was beginning to get very angry. Of all the systems on the ship. Why did I have to have the system that would fail? The air pressure went down to 96 lb's. I figured that down the line to the guns the air pressure would be at least two lb's lower. Mr. Wentworth called me over to the telephone and told me to explain to the damage control officer what the trouble was. I told him that the 200 lb. air pressure was down to 96 lbs and was close to shutting off the air to the guns. I had just talked with the No. 4 engine room by our JV phone and found out that the 3000 lb. air compressor in that engine room wasn't running. This 3000 lb. air was used to cushion the recoil when the main guns were firing, and also to replenish the 200 lb. gas ejection system, when needed. During battle these lines, which circled the ship were isolated so that the forward two sixteen inch turrets were separated from the after turret, the same with the 200 lb. gas ejection system. All of the action seemed to be on the starboard side, and the forward sixteen inch turrets were firing steady, as we were chasing the enemy ships. The forward diesel and air compressors were supplying these guns with gas ejection air.

I was explaining this to the damage control officer, when a strange voice interrupted our conversation, and asked? "What's the solution?" I quickly responded, "open up the H.P. 3000 lb. air line, as the H.P. air compressor in the No. Four engine room wasn't running. He said "Do it". I called the forward electrical distribution board, where the air valve was located and had it opened. My gas ejection air started to rise. I informed the damage control officer, and we began firing again. However during this interlude, we were hit again on the port bow. We were lucky as the Marines that had occupied this area, had just left the area. We soon sank the ships we were chasing.

At noon we broke off the engagement, and started to feed the crew. Steak and eggs. I thought this was unusual, as we had never done this on the destroyer I was on. We didn't eat until the battle was over. I remember one day we didn't eat until after 1700 navy time. (5 PM) Mr. Wentworth told me to stay put, he would bring me my meal. He was afraid we would start firing again, and I wouldn't be able to get below in time. When the dinner hour was over, he brought me down some soda crackers. He was unable to bring me anything else.

I am going to stop here and let you read the Ships log for this battle. On the fiftieth anniversary of this event, I went aboard the U.S.S. Massachusetts in Fall River Mass. It was November 8,]992. The ship is now a memorial, and part of the Battleship Cove Memorial Park. I went to this event, and met one of the CORP. officers. He gave me a copy of the ships log, for Nov. 8, 1942. The log is some what different from my description. The yeomen who typed this log was wrong about some things also, In his haste he has Turret 1 mixed up with turret 10. The evidence is readily visible when you go aboard ship and see the scare on No. 10 turret.

USS MASSACHUSETTS BB59

Sunday, Nov. 8 1942 Ships log

Time	
0545	General Quarters.
0550	Set Material condition Zed.
0555	Damage Control maned and ready.
0604	Ammunition and power up to all guns.
0617	Catapulted one plane to port
0620	Catapulted one plane to stbd.
0623	Seven red flares off the port quarter.
0634	Paint locker flooded with carbon dioxide.
0651	Anti-aircraft has opened fire on- planes from the beach.
0656	Message from our plane, 'we have encountered hostile aircraft.
0657	Aircraft approaching.
0658	One of our planes coming in on our starboard bow, hostile aircraft are following it.
0659	Open fire on hostile aircraft.
0701	Our Destroyers have opened fire on enemy planes.

0702	Have opened fire on planes, (light bombers)
0703	The Jean Bart has opened fire upon us.
0705	All turrets loaded.
0705	One of our planes down, dead ahead.
0706	Change to flank speed.
0715	Numerous bombs being dropped on us- all near misses
0717	"No flame, a lot of smoke, it looks good", a report from one of our talkers.
0717	Torpedo plane approaching from the East.
0719	Opening up on EL Hank. Fort at entrance to harbor.
0720	Planes off the port bow.
0721	Enemy planes approaching on port beam.
0722	Our planes on port beam.
0724	All batteries have been firing steady.
0725	Dive bombers attacking our cruiser.
0725	Enemy planes approaching.
0728	Fire started on jetty at Casablanca.
0736	Jean Barts' range 29,000 yd.
0737	Ships on the horizon, 148 degree's relative.
0740	Last salvo looked like hit on Jean Bart.
0741	Have ceased fire on Jean Bart. Looks like fire on either Jetty or Jean Bart.
0741.5	Bart is not burning-pier is burning.
0744	Landing barges off the port bow approx. range 10,000 yd. EL Hank still firing. (belay) is not firing.
0754	Our soldiers have captured one sector.
0755	Enemy aircraft on port beam. Two motored bombers.
0756	Man injured in turret three. Injury not serious.
0759	No firing from EL Hank for some time
0800	USS Tuscaloosa out of commission.
0801	Unidentified warship bearing 326 degrees
0807	Direct Hit on Target. Announcement from the chaplain on the bridge. An enemy cruiser is firing on us. Our guns are firing back, and we hit our target with three sixteen inch projectiles. There was a big explosion and the ship was engulfed in smoke. When the smoke cleared there was nothing left.
0810	Plane approaching 205 degree's
0811	Jean Bart firing secondary battery.
0817	Enemy submarines leaving the harbor (2).
0826	Leak in fire main on flag bridge.
0827	Shells landed off port bow.
0829	French blowing up ammunition dumps on the other side of town.
0832	Unidentified ships bearing 95 degrees∞
0834	Cease firing signal is in the air.
0835	Execute the cease firing signal.
0839	Going out to pick up our planes.
0845	Standby to recover plane. Going after cruiser attacking our transports. One enemy shell went through our colors - colors we went into commission with.
0909	Enemy cruisers dead ahead.
0910	Augusta and Brooklyn firing.
0911	Over ten planes on port side.
0912	Augusta and New York firing at unknown object.
0914	Destroy enemy: Cruisers between Casablanca and Fedala. The Main Battery is firing constantly, just as fast as the guns can be loaded. There is a constant roar of gun fire.
0916	Three French Cruisers bearing 200 Degree's Fired on Cruisers., Cruisers returning fire.
0922	Believe to have a hit on cruiser- it is smoking.
0923	Casualty in turret III (high pressure Airline).
0924	Believe two cruisers hit.

0925	Much white smoke coming out of one cruiser.
	Belay 0923 entry.
0927	Wichita and Tuscaloosa firing.
0928	Six planes over head - friendly.
0929	Shell hit 300 yards off our beam.
0930	One shell passed our ship.
0934	Two cruisers to starboard smoking badly.
	Many misses on all sides of us.
0941	Two cruisers firing at us. Near misses - matter of feet.
0943	Two cruisers hit
0945	Short at frame 81, shrapnel falling but no apparent damage.
0945	Hit on a super Destroyer.
0946	Ten planes off the port bow- friendly.
0947	Two near misses on the port beam. Down in the Forward Diesel my 200 lb. air pressure was down to around 95 or 96 lb. and I was forced to do some thing. I was at this time calling damage control and telling the damage control officer he would have to call the bridge and have them stop firing, as the automatic air valve would shut the air off if the air pressure went below 90 lb.
0950	Small wake in the water, 205 degree's
0951	Another Cruiser, 254 degree's
0952	Range 22050 yards.
0956	Ship on horizon bearing 335 degree's
0959	Hit on Port bow, abreast of turret two.
1000	Unit three reports a hit in turret -A-208-L
	No causalities, or fires.
1001	Torpedo bomber coming in on port beam
1003	Enemy cruiser sinking.
1005	Torpedo wakes on port bow. (3).
1007	One miss.
1008	All misses, by ten feet.
	Launched by plane, (One Torpedo).
1010	One Cruiser stopped.
1011	Fire in A-208—L
1011	Submarine on port bow, 207 degrees
1014	General repair has one hose playing on a fire at frame 64, main deck port side.
1015	One of many cruisers sunk.
1021	Torpedo wake on port bow.
1022	Missed.
1025	Opening all circle Zed fittings, (belay).
1025	One of our planes above us.
1026	Two Cruisers engaging the USS Brooklyn and USS Augusta.
1028	Destroyer leader is firing on us.
1032	Range 19800 yards.
1035	Three ships firing at us.
1036	Range 20150 yards.
1038	Both of our planes down, (out of gas).
1040	Range 20400 yards.
1041	Lieut. Doerflinger has]5 minutes gasoline supply.
1042	Turret I temporarily out of commission. Turret III has two guns out of commission.
1050	Small piece of canvas burning on main deck, Fr.112
1051	Quick acting door by Executive Officers' office carried away.
1051	Two near misses, (fifty yards away.)
1054	Cruisers now in range of 5" guns.
1055	Five planes approaching from forward, port bow, friendly.
1055	Near miss (25 yards on starboard beam).
1057	Hit aft of Conn. on starboard beam.
1100	Destroyer coming in very fast.
1101	We are firing at one cruiser, the rest are in a smoke screen, and this one has come out firing. (Aloft observer).

1104	Transmitter room for Radar is becoming warm.
1105	Hauling out for the present.
1107	Hit on Group 13 guns under control, no casualties. Fire under control.
1108	Stand by to pick up plane
1111	Frame 105 - air line pierced
1113	Smoke in third deck passage way & B-3
1115	Belay 1113
1116	Medium pressure air line to Mount 1 leaking badly
1120	Ship on the horizon
	Black object coming out of water, 2000 yards.
1126	Belay 1125
1126	Be prepared to recover plane to port.
1130	Plane is out of water
1133	Plane is secured ton catapult
1136	Plane in water bearing 333 degrees, appears to be our plane
1141	leak in high pressure air line, fr. 104.5 stbd. 2nd deck
1144	Keeping recovery gear rigged.
1146	Four planes coming over
1148	Many planes coming over
1153	All repair parties opening unnecessary hatches for Watch #1 to eat.
1158	Permission granted to open engineers head
1202	Permission granted to cut in air , steam , and water to the galley
1205	cut in steam to galley
1210	Odor of Formaldehyde coming from amidships battle dressing station
1214	Two ships on horizon approaching, bearing 80 degrees
1218	Permission to cut in flushing water to head, main deck
1224	Degaussing gear is ruptured, fr. 46 port, 2nd deck A208L and there is juice on it. General repair notified
1230	Plane dropped depth charge
1255	B-32-F practically all water, believed to leaking from shrapnel hole.
1305	Two French Cruisers and a Destroyer on the horizon
1310	General Quarters
1313	Repair with out lights
1323	Repair to, catapult plane to starboard
1325	Range 28,000 yards.
1327	Starboard catapult is out of order. Shifting plane to port catapult
1328	Plan to engage Fort EL HANK
1330	Ship bearing 35 degrees Smoking badly
1335	Ready to catapult plane
1336	Plane catapulted to port.
1339	Stand by to fire to starboard.
1339	Firing at Destroyer leader
1340	EL HANK opened fire
1340.5	Several near misses on Starboard quarter.
1342	EL Hank firing from three different places.
1344	Range to EL Hank 19100 yards.
1345	Our last shot right on.
1350	Near misses again.
134.5	Near misses.
1347	Dive bombers dead ahead. (friendly).
1350	Cease firing.
1350	Near misses.
1351	Conn to control "Search for other targets"
1354	Cut in Power to mount 1.
1355	Ship in entrance to harbor apparently on fire. (French Cruiser
1402	Cruiser appears to be beached.
1409	Black smoke on horizon, bearing 146∞.
1415	first can of sardines opened in damage control central.
1417	All stations send watch 11 to mess hall.

Time	
1423	Commander Field figures mean draft to be 34"1"
1433	Letting aircraft attack shore bases so that we can move in closer.
1446	Salvo from USS Tuscaloosa.
1447	Salvo from USS Wichita.
1500	The USS Wichita's last salvo on a cruiser gave it a 45 degree list
1500	EL Hank is in flames.
1504	Investigating strange destroyer on stbd. beam.
1506	Range on EL Hank 48000 yards.
1513	Now making our final approach on EL Hank.
1514	Right gun of turret 11 out of commission.
1515	General quarters, prepare for battle again.
1516	Cut power in Mount 1.
1517	Set condition Zed.
1518	Lieut. Doerflinger reports there is no activity in side the harbor.
1520	Range 55000 yards.
1522	Condition Zed is set.
1527	Two submarines have surfaced and are heading into, Casablanca.
1533	Range 22.9 miles to EL Hank.
1543	Ship sighted 21000 yd. off port bow.
1542	Enemy Destroyer headed for open sea.
1546	Six planes over head to stbd. (friendly)
1547	Plane coming in on stbd. side.
1548	Cut in power to mount 1.
1551	Will pass 30,000 yd. from EL Hank.
1555	Cut power off to mount 1.
1556	Turret three standing by to fire.
1556	Turret two standing by to fire.
1556	Range 31000 yd.
1559	Five planes approaching from port quarter.
1601	Smoking ship on horizon at 330 degrees
1693	AA fire, bearing 56 degree's from shore
1603	Stand by to pick up plane.
1604	Enemy Cruiser just caught fire at entrance to harbor
1606	Last salvo hit military store house at El Hank
1610	Secure from General Quarters. "Whew"
	Battle for today finished now heading out to sea to lick our wounds.

USS MASSACHUSETTS BB59 NOV, 8,1942

Recapitulation of expended Ammunition

	Turret			
	1	2	3	Total
Rounds expended	276	251	261	788
Rounds remaining	84	202	99	385
Weight of shell	2700 lb.			
Weight of each load	3262 lb.			
fired (lb.)	800,312	818,762	851,382	2,460,465
Before action	360	453	360	1173

USS MASSACHUSETTS BB 59

Tuesday Nov. 10, 1942 Ships Log

Time	
0900	General Quarters.
0905	Set condition Zed.
0914	Damage control maned and ready.
0922	Condition Zed set.
0926	Bearing on Casablanca Harbor 112∞.

0937	Range to EL Hank 35,500 yd.
0943.5	Range to EL Hank 36,500 yd.
1006	EL Hank 126 degrees
1010	USS Texas and USS New York are now with us.
1013	Friendly planes dead ahead. (PBY's)
1014	Message from USS Texas plane, we are encountering no anti-aircraft fire at all. Unable to find any target of opportunity.
1021.5	Investigating white smoke on horizon.
1031	Range on grain elevator near EL Hank is 39,501 yd.
1038	USS Wainright is going into Casablanca Harbor. (Destroyer)
1106.5	AA fire seems to be coming from the beach.
1110.5	USS Ranger had four torpedoes fired at her-all missed.
1110.5	Range on EL Hank 41,700 yd. Bearing 183 degree's
1121	French Destroyer off Casablanca that may be firing.
1121	USS Wainright has several submarine contacts.
1129	Columns of smoke rising from the city.
1130	Wake across bow- 800 yards.
1135	One of our Destroyers appears to be burning on horizon.
1136	Our Destroyer firing on beach, 261∞
1137	USS Texas has opened fire.
1138	Considerable smoke coming from USS Augusta.
1139	USS New York is firing.
1139	Destroyer is firing.
1139	They are firing at destroyers, some one laying smoke screen.
1140.5	Ships firing on port beam.
1141	AA fire from our battleships.
1141.5	They are firing from the beach now.
1142.5	Appears as though the Jean Bart is firing.
1143	(Belay Jean Bart firing) Cruiser inside Harbor is shooting.
1144	Looks as though the Jean Bart is firing her after 6".
1145	Bearing Jean Bart 155∞-looks as though Bart is firing 16"
1146	Jean Bart appears to have been hit.
1146	Smoke over one of the battleships.
1148.5	EL Hank has opened fire.
1149	Another salvo from Jean Bart.
1150	Another salvo from Jean Bart.
1155	Large yellow splashes around USS Augusta, bearing 220∞
1157	USS Augusta signaling us.
1157	Fishing boat returning back towards harbor.
1200	Chow for watch 1.
1201	Range to EL HANK 32,000 yd.
1205	All hands back to battle stations
1210	Pipe down chow for watch 11 at 1230.
1220	Jean Bart has started to fire again
1222	Be prepared to make full speed at 1230.
1226	Range on Jean Bart 37,780 yd.
1229	French Destroyer standing out of harbor
1231	Plane coming bearing 025 degree's
1232	Be prepared to launch one aircraft at 1300.
1233	Pipe down chow for watch 11.
1251	Expedite dinner.
1302	Leak in fire plug 1-64, not serious.
1307	Pipe down chow for watch 111.
1341	All hands who have not eaten dinner lay below to the mess hall immediately.
1346	All the crew of turret 111 man your battle station on the double
1352	Keep, a sharp look out for all fishing boats
1358	Signal in the air to change course and head into the beach
1402.5	Galley is through serving.

1406	USS Wainright reports small boat, 335 degrees.	
1411.5	Bearing on EL HANK, 340 degrees	
1415	USS New York bearing 255 degrees	
1415	Zed set in turret three.	
1417	Started zig-zagging.	
1418	Plane on 18 degrees relative is making recognition signal.	
1425	Cease zig-zagging and resume course	
1426	Small fishing craft dead ahead.	
1433.5	USS Wainright reports enemy bearing 200 degrees	
1434	Fishing boat on starboard bow covered.	
1436	All personnel clear of mess halls.	
1446	Object bearing 60 degrees on horizon, Destroyer investigating.	
1446	Object appears to be a ship, we are headed for it now.	
1446.5	Destroyer going after fishing boat.	
1448	Ship on port bow is calling us.	
1454	Destroyer on starboard quarter is up to fishing boat.	
1457	Wake bearing 104 degrees	
1506	Secure from general quarters, set condition yoke. Watch 11 on duty.	

That's it for today.

A few days later we were on our way back to Norfolk, Va. to load ammunition. At this time the heads of all departments met in the ward room, for damage reports. I wasn't invited as the first class machinist mate from the after diesel was the head of my department. I learned from Mr. Wentworth that my name came up several times. First, I was to get an advancement in rating to first class machinist mate. Then some body remarked that I had just been rated a month before, so they took it away. Then somebody thought I should get a general court martial, for opening that valve on the H.P. air line. That was a Condition Zed designation valve, (closed during battle). Then Mr. Wentworth said, "Hey wait a minute, I was in charge of that station, if anybody gets a court martial, it'll be me." For his punishment he was transferred.

A year later we were in the South Pacific, It was just before we were to retake the Gilbert Islands. The Chief engineering officer on the ship showed me a letter from the Bureau of Ships in Washington, D.C. The letter stated that what I had done was the proper thing to do. That all ships of this class would henceforth go to general quarters with this air valve open. He remarked, "That will be a feather in your cap". I asked him for a copy of that letter, but he said no, I have to keep it for my records. There is more to this story, I'll get back to it later.

On our trip back across the Atlantic, I was with some friends, and we were going down to the No. 2 pump room, as a crap game was going on down there. I started but, something gave me a nudge on my shoulder, it irritated me, then a thought came to me, What about that girl up there in Maine? You had better set down and write her a letter. It reminded me of my mother, making me do something, I'd rather put off until tomorrow, and never doing it. I wrote a hasty letter and mailed it. I didn't expect an answer.

We loaded ammunition in Norfolk, Virginia, and then went up to Boston, Mass. It was just before Thanksgiving. I had my first assignment as a shore patrol man in Boston. I rode around in a police cruiser. The officer took me into the Old Howard. (The Old Howard was a strip tease show house, with a bad reputation). Then we went to his precinct. He soon came out and we raced through the streets of Boston, with his siren going full blast. He muttered something about a fire.

We arrived at the COCONUT Grove Restaurant. Somebody was breaking a hole in a brick type window. I came along and went immediately into the hole, and found a body on the floor. I picked the body up and discovered he was still alive. I carried him out to a hotel across the street, with my "Peacoat" wrapped around him. Then went back across the street, and into the building and picked up his girl friend, she gave a shudder as I picked her up. I took her out and laid her on the ground, then went back in for another. I carried people out of that building until midnight. By then we had sheets, and we would roll the body onto the sheet, then two of us would carry it out to a railway express truck, and load them into the truck. After a while I was asked to get into the truck and stack the bodies up like cord wood sticks. I did that for a while then had to get out of their, as I was getting sick. I was guarding one of the back doors, when Mayor Curly came along and wanted to go in and take a look at the mess inside. It was around midnight, and I was getting tired, dirty, and couldn't find that policeman I was with, so I went back to the ship. The next morning the newspapers estimated their were around five hundred people that died in that fire.

The next day I received a letter from Vera. She was visiting her cousins in Tewksbury, Mass. and she gave me directions on how to get out there. I didn't realize it took four hours to get there. The time spent at the Bernsson house was worth the long ride out there. I fell head over heels in love. I would go out there, and would be completely consumed with her innocence. The other three girls, (Barbara, and Ella, and Eleanor) wanted me to bring some sailors out with me. I brought three carefully selected guys with me, with strict instructions on their conduct. Dec. flew by and before I knew it, we were headed south, through the Panama Canal.

I am getting ahead of myself. When we pulled in to Boston Harbor, from Norfolk, Va. I was given the task to remove the cylinder heads on the Forward Emergency diesel Generator engine. This was a major job. I was to inspect the cylinder wall for signs of rust, and pitting. This was from the incident with water on our trip to Africa. Word got around about what was going on down in the forward diesel. The engineering officers would come down, and ask me how things were going, and I would show them the engine and reassure them. There was no damage to the engine. However, in other parts of the ship, some people were upset that I was getting so much attention.

A new Warrant officer came aboard, in place of Mr. Wentworth. He wanted to make an impression on the other engineering officers. He made a drawing of a water temperature control valve on the emergency diesel engine. Actually, he copied it from a blue print. He said he had made a modification on it. He came to me and asked what I thought of it. I didn't want to get involved with him, so I said it looked all right to me. I could see that it was an exact copy, and was frightened, he could cause me a lot of trouble. When he took it to the other engineering officers, they immediately recognized it as a copy. Was he ever mad at me. He claimed, That I had led him on about the drawing. In short I was on his shit list from then on.

All this time we had in Boston that December, I was in a dream world, between Vera, and that diesel engine, I was in heaven. I loved what I was doing, and the beauty of it all, "I was my own boss" I had control of everything that was going on around me. I put the engine back together and it ran perfectly. I learned how to put the engine on the line, and build it up to full load. The engine was made by Cooper Bessemer Manufacturing Co.

When I went out to visit Vera, we always had a nice supper, at Jack Bernssen's house. Then after supper we would go for a walk until it was time to leave. As we waited at the buss stop, Vera would put her arms under my "Pea" coat and hug me, and I would kiss her. When I left there I couldn't see straight. She sure got under my skin.

The end of Dec. we got under way. We ran into a bad storm off the coast of North Carolina, "Cape Hatteras". Down in the Forward Diesel you could feel the forward part of the ship shudder, and act like a giant spring, when those huge waves hit our bow. Going through the Panama Canal, my crew and I were in the forward wiring trunk hauling an electrical cable from the forward distribution board to the No. 1 turret. The bad storm had short circuited the main feeder cable, to No. 1 turret. The navy had flown a new cable from the states to Colon, Panama. My crew spent all of our trip through the Panama Canal, down below working. We hauled the new cable, from our Forward Diesel compartment through a wiring trunk up to No. 1 turret. This time the Captain had everybody on deck, and commended my crew on our hard work, installing that cable. He gave us special liberty in Balboa, on the Pacific side of the canal. The only people on the ship to get liberty in Balboa. I went a shore and took back with me a Balboa silver dollar, half dollar, and a quarter. I liked these coins as they had a nice image of Desoto on them.
As we set out into the Pacific ocean a large bird perched on our main mast. We looked upon it as a good omen. Everybody on board ship had an adventurous feeling about going into the south Pacific except me. I felt terrible, as I knew what was ahead of us. About a month later we entered, Noumea New Caledonia. What a wild place that was, it was unbearably hot. As you get near the war zone all ships go into general quarters mornings and evenings, also some times you can spend hours at your general quarters station. Then the hot weather can sap your energy, and keep you from eating. It wasn't long and we were taking salt tablets. I sweat so much, that under my arm pits, my under shirt turned reddish orange. I couldn't sleep in my bunk, as I would sweat all night, and in the morning,

I would be laying in a puddle of sweat. I tried to get the officers to let me take the heating coils out of the ventilation system, and clean the dirt out. They said no, we were in the war zone, and we couldn't take the chance. I never slept in my bunk after that. I slept on the deck plates down in the forward diesel.

One Sunday we started to go ashore for a beach party. We could go swimming. We got about half way there, and we had an air attack. We had to scramble to get back to the ship. The ship had gotten underway. By the time I got aboard, I couldn't get to my battle station, the forward diesel. I made up my mind not to leave the ship again in hostile territory.

Mail call was the event of the month. I read and reread Vera's letters. I kept them in my pocket until the next mail call or until I wore them out. I was writing every chance I could get, What could I say? I didn't do anything except stand my watches. I couldn't tell her where or what we were doing. I just dreamed of the future, and told her how much I loved her, and missed her.

Down in the forward diesel I was having my troubles. I was so much in love, that I failed to realize what was going on, until it was too late. My division officer had a lot of confidence in me as a repairman. I was called upon to do all kinds of repair work. At one time I was asked to realign a gun director, up on the superstructure. The gun director was on the port side just aft of the bridge. Everybody could see us working up there. The gun director was a couple minutes in degree's off from center. It was my job to remove the hold down bolts, from the director mounting plate. Shift the whole director a degree in minute's, then have the gunner's mate tell me if that was enough. I then had to set a new position for the locating dowel, and bolt the director back down again.

The next thing I was called upon to over haul our three thousand lb. air compressor in the No. 4 engine room. This compressor was under the control of a 2/class machinist mate by the name of Charles Cutler. This was a new machine, and Cutler hadn't adjusted the individual cylinder oiler's, as the manufacture had recommended. He had given the oiler's too much oil, and the oil had exploded much the same as a diesel engine would. A diesel engine explodes at 1000 lb's., and this compressor worked at 3000 lb's. These oiler's had sight glasses that you could watch as the machine ran, and you adjusted them by sight. They moved him out of there while I worked on his machine. To do these jobs, you were required to work continuously until the job was done. This job took three days and nights to accomplish. Next the automatic shut off valve to the No. 10 anti- aircraft gun mount hadn't worked since the battle at Casablanca. One day I was ordered to go and fix that valve. Cutler went with me. He had fixed that valve several times before, and each time it continued to leak. His problem was, he was twisting that little 1/4 inch nipple too tight, and it cracked. It worked after I got through with it. Looking back on it now, Cutler probably didn't like me at all. During this time, there was one First Class machinist mate rating that would be awarded to some 2/nd class machinist mate that summer. To qualify for this rating, all A Div. machinist mates were required to be qualified in the various stations in the main engine room. Which I was doing on my time. The A Division warrant officer, (I have forgotten his name) told me that to pass this examination for first class, I would have to make a drawing of a steam line expansion joint. He named this fitting by manufactures name, which was supposed to be different from the drawing in our first class machinist mates manual. One of the chief machinist mates in the engine room liked me, he asked me to put in for his engine room, and get out of that hot house of the forward diesel. He gave me a brochure on that particular expansion joint. Now I was the only one on board ship that knew how to draw that expansion joint. During this time I was standing oiler watches in the engine room with Douglas Odom from Monhegan Island. He said he knew Vera's family and where they lived. He told me a lot about Ingraham's Hill. I really enjoyed talking with him. I liked the engine room, but hated to leave the forward diesel. The forward diesel offered more technical knowledge for me, including Electrical experience, with the Electrical distribution board right there. I was my own boss in the forward diesel, and that was hard to give up. I had control here, and I felt that I needed to know that the air compressors were working, and in good order. I had something to do here every day, and that's the way I am.

One day I put one of my firemen to work, chipping rust, and painting a fire and flushing pump in the forward diesel. It wasn't a bad job, in fact it was rather easy. I had started to do it myself when this warrant officer told me, I shouldn't be doing that. I should have one of my firemen do it. I assigned this fireman to do this job. That was easy enough, then I went down to No. 2 pump room, to check on something. Usually I had to keep track of the packing glands, and pump bearings on the fire and flushing pumps down there. They could get very hot, and I didn't want anything to happen to them. On my way back to the forward diesel I catch this same guy up on deck. I asked him, "what are you doing up on deck?" He was real belligerent, and told me Shinover MM 1/c from the after diesel, had told him not to pay any attention to me, and go up on deck and get some fresh air. I told him I would put him on report. He told me to go ahead, it won't do me any good, as it would have to go through Shinovers hands first. I let it go from there, to hell with the pump.

For awhile I had the eight to twelve watches, when this warrant officer would come down to the forward diesel and give me hell about some valve that didn't work, or some packing gland on a pump that was running hot. I was to see that they were fixed before I went off watch. This would happen just as I was going off watch. I usually wound up working a couple more hours after my watch was over. I would have to give him a written report, that the whole forward diesel, the two pump rooms, the air systems, and the after diesel were in first class condition, before I could be relieved from my watch.

One day just after lunch, I was getting some air and sun. This was a luxury for me as I spent almost all of my time down in the forward diesel. I even slept on the deck plates so as to be on my battle station in case we were called to general quarters. The main steam generators lost the load, and the emergency diesels had to kick in. My generator in the forward diesel failed to start. The engine failed because the over speed trip on the flywheel shut off the fuel to the engine. I knew what was wrong, and had instructed my men on watch to keep an eye on this. It took a few minutes. To get the engine started. Then Shinover would come down from the after diesel, and he would readjust this over speed trip. Then tell me not to touch it afterwards. When he left, I tried to start the engine, and it tripped. I readjusted it. Somebody snitched, and I was given another lecture, and told to leave it alone. It was no use to argue with him, and as I was responsible for the equipment. I waited until a twelve to four watch, and readjusted it again. As our station was next to the evaporators, I began to suspect one of these men, as the next day Shinover MM 1/c was back readjusting that over speed trip. I should have gone over his head, and had a talk with my division officer. I thought about it, but was afraid. I knew that when these guy's were after you their wasn't much I could do about it. I was getting too close to getting that first class rating, and if I got it, Shinover would be in a different position. He wouldn't be able to come down to the forward diesel and spend all morning lecturing.

One Sat. morning, I was told to teach my men everything I knew about our equipment. I started with doing preventative maintenance on our 200 lb. air compressors, the most important machines in the forward diesel. I called the control engine room and received permission to disable one of my air compressors. I took one of the four valve cages out of the cylinder head, and very carefully replaced the valve cover. All the time explaining why I took such safety precautions. I was teaching them how to care for this valve, when I got a call from my div. officer. He asked me if I knew anything about a Buda diesel engine, and if I could over haul it. I replied, that although I had never overhauled a Buda diesel, I had watched the men on the U.S.S. Oklahoma do it, and I would like to try it. He told me, that we had only one overhaul kit, and I should be careful, not to spoil anything.

The engine was in the aviation work shop. I worked all afternoon, (Friday), Saturday, and Sunday afternoon. We had taken the engine all apart, and had replaced the cylinder sleeves, main bearings, pistons, and rod bearings. We got up to the cylinder head, and I had ground the valves in, (by hand), and had installed the valves and valve springs. My next step would be to seat the energy valves. I got a phone call. One of my firemen in the forward diesel. He told me I should get down there right away. When Cutler MM2/c had come around on his watch, and he was to roll over all idle machinery. He couldn't roll over the air compressor that we had worked on before I went to work on the Buda Diesel. He had tried to turn it over by hand, and it would only go so far, and he had to turn it over the other way. Then he pushed the start button, and it went klunk. That alone was a no, no. You never do that, the policy was to investigate the problem first. I could never understand why they were able to charge me with this accident. The chief engineer, told me that I was in charge of the forward diesel, and the one responsible. I instructed the 2/c machinist mate "Tate" how to install the energy cell valves, then the correct torque to use on the cylinder head studs, and the proper sequence for tightening these head bolts. I told him I would be right back anyway. There were only six of these valves, one for each cylinder. They controlled an energy cell in the cylinder head, and were used for starting the engine. The valves were controlled by an arm connected to the valve stem, and a rod connected to the arms. When you pulled the arm out, it would turn the valves and close off the energy cell. This gave the engine cylinders a higher compression pressure, which would aid in starting the engine. With these valves closed the engine would belch black smoke out of it. Until you opened the energy cell by pushing this rod in. I showed him how to put it together. Then left for the forward diesel. When I arrived the fireman told me what

Cutler had done. He said the compressor went over and clunk it stopped. I took one of the valve cages out, and found a bolt inside, and the bolt had put a hole into the piston. I was at a complete loss, as to how this could happen. The compressor was all right when I left it. I had turned it over by hand to make sure everything was all right before I left. That was part of my procedure, and had been ever since I had been doing preventative maintenance on my machines.

At that time I couldn't think of anybody that would sabotage any of my machines. I thought we were fighting a war against the Japanese. It was hard enough as it was, without fighting each other. All I could think about, at that time, was how I could fix it. I figured that who ever done this was smart, this was the opportune time to do it. He knew where I was. The officers arrived, and looked at the damage. The chief engineer told me to fix it. Then come up to his office. I patched the piston. I still have that piece of piston that I removed. I only put on a temporary patch, as I expected a new piston in a week or two. The new piston would be flown out from the states. Mean while the man working on the Buda diesel had finished, and had put the engine in the boat, and were trying it out. They called me on deck where we could watch the boat on its trial run. The engine smoked, and they wanted to know why. I said, "Why didn't the engineer push in the energy cell rod, and open the energy cells. Shinover said they had already done that. I told him Tate had put this part of the engine together, and he should have checked those valves before putting the head on. This was too much for me. I still didn't realize there were people out there who were going after me.

The chief engineer was still investigating the incident in the forward diesel. I went into his office to discuss it. When I sat down, he suddenly motioned for me not to speak and follow him. We went top side and walked back and forth over the quarter deck. He wanted to know of anybody who might have it in for me. I told him I had no idea, but would think about it for a day or two, and then let him know. This was a bad thing and I wanted to be sure of who it might be, as he could be put to death. I thought of the two people who were giving me such a hard time, (Shinover, and the warrant officer) but I was afraid. I didn't think I could run the emergency diesel generators with out Shinover's help. I needed him. I was afraid, those people could get me in real trouble. I gave him the names of a couple of guy's that might have done it, or were in on it. I expected him to interrogate them. The first thing I knew they were transferred.

On one of our walks, the chief engineer showed me a letter he had received from the bureau of ships. It said that, what I had done during the battle at Casablanca, was the right thing to have done. That the battleships, U.S.S. South Dakota, U.S.S. Indiana, U.S.S. Alabama, and U.S.S. Massachusetts were to change the classification of this valve to be open during battle. The engineering officer said that would be a feather in my cap. He added, when a chance comes by for a break, I'll see to it that you will get it. What that break was I never knew. When we got underway this time, I was removed from the forward diesel and assigned to the No. Four engine room, and the 3000 lb. air compressor would be my responsibility. That was to be my battle station. I was heart sick, and didn't care whether school kept or not. During general quarters, I would go down to the pump room and drink coffee and smoke. I didn't go near the compressor. We were at sea for over three months, and during that time we invaded the Gilbert Islands, and bombarded some other island, then we came back in to Efate Island in the New Hebride. During this time at sea, we were at general quarters for long periods of time, and the crew got awful touchy. If you were going down a passage way and accidentally bumped another sailor, you found your self in a fist fight, we were so up tight, and bored, it was hard to say anything good about anybody. We were to start a round the clock repair of all equipment. I was assigned a little service air compressor, for preventative maintenance. I was to renew the cooling water piping. I sent one of my men up to get three pieces of half inch copper tubing. He came back and said they told him, they were out of half inch copper pipe. The next morning we had captains inspection. We were standing on the quarter deck In front of the whole "A" division. When Shinover MM1/c started to give me hell for not renewing those pipe lines, In front of everybody. Again I had a tear in my eye. I turned away from him and looked skyward. I said to myself, "God if I ever get out of this South Pacific, and back to the north American continent, I shall never leave it. The "A" division officers were right in front of us, when this happened. After inspection, I was assigned shore patrol duty. I spent the after noon trying to keep peace between the battleship crews. I remember the sixth division officer telling his men not to take any guff from the U.S.S. Washington crews about shooting too close to their fan tail during target practice. They were a cocky bunch of guys as they had the distinction of sinking a Japanese battleship, and we were also cocky, because we had sunk the battleship Jean Bart.

When I came back to the ship, one of my firemen, told me there was a transfer to a navy advanced diesel school up for grabs. That the "A" division officer was looking for me. I went right up to see him. He first asked me how much sea duty I had. I explained that I had 39 months of sea duty. He asked me if I would like to go to the diesel school. He said you know you will never make first class on this ship, and the diesel school will last only six weeks and then I could be back out there and be making the next invasion. If I stayed on board the Mass. I could possibly survive the war. I told him I couldn't stay anywhere I couldn't make an advancement in rating, and that I'd take the transfer. He said, "I suppose you will get married, I thought that was funny, until I realized he had been reading my letters all this time to Vera. Before I end my time on board the U.S.S. Mass. I have to mention a little adventure I had on a Torpedo boat. We were in Noumea New Caledonia. My division officer asked me to volunteer to go engineer on this torpedo boat, as their engineer was sick. I volunteered, on condition that I could get back aboard when I got back. I went, and found out that it wasn't such a good idea. I had to ride down in the engine room, and wear a crash helmet with ear plugs. I had set on a iron seat much like a farm tractor, with the instrument panel in front of me. The captain started the engine, shifted it and set the speed. I couldn't see anything, and I didn't do anything, this was awful. The engines were three, sixteen cylinder P 40 aircraft engines. I could set there and see the high octane gas tanks. I figured if we were ever hit I could get a good burn. I was glad to get back aboard the battleship. Another thing I didn't like, they didn't have any food aboard, we had to bum food whereever we were. We seemed to do our work at night. One morning we made a high speed run against the fleet. I was told afterward that we would have been blown out of the water. That was enough for me, I requested permission to return to the ship. Another thing that makes this interesting. The crew told me that the captain was a rich yachtsman from Boston. I remember the engines were not synchronized and were in a bad way. I often wondered how they managed to get them started. There is no mention of my going aboard this vessel in my service records.

We stayed in Noumea around three months, then moved up to Efate an Island in the New Hebrides. It was a small lagoon surrounded by coconut trees. We used to pull in there for a short stay for repairs. We spent most of our time at sea. It was very frustrating, we would make full speed runs north to the Solomons and arrive just a few minutes too late, for the battle. These runs north were hard on us as we were straining all the time the engines were run at full speed. I was beginning to feel the strain when my head began to ache, and when I had to go up the ladder to get to the pump rooms I could feel a cord on my neck that would pull. It gave me a head ache.

When we were in Efate, I was able to go on a beach party, where we would be issued two cans of beer, and some macaroni salad. The natives from the Islands would come around in their dugout canoes, and try to sell us love birds, with home made cages. We didn't buy, because we knew that they would die the first time we fired our guns. We would go swimming on these beach parties. I used to tell these guy's not to put their head under water, as they would get a fungus infection. They didn't listen and some of them got a very serious ear infection, and were transferred back to the states.

I left the ship the next morning, it was around the end of Dec. 1943. I boarded an Australian freighter, carrying fresh meat and vegetables. I had breakfast aboard. It was the best food I had eaten in years. I tried for seconds, but was to late, it was all gone. The ship was refrigerated and I sat on the deck all morning in the shade, where it was cool. The coolest I had been in a year. We landed in Esprito Santo's, the northern most island in the New Hebrides. The war was moving ever northward, and this place showed, where at one time it was loaded with Marines. The islands ships company didn't like us state side sailors, and they would line us up under the coconut trees for muster. The threat of a coconut falling from a tree was ever present. One afternoon, I was setting in my tent, when I heard somebody crying. I looked around and saw a sailor on his bed crying. I went over to talk to him to see if I could be of some help. He told me he was crying because he couldn't forget his experience on board the aircraft carrier U.S.S. Yorktown. During the battle of Midway, he was on a destroyer, that sent a rescue party aboard the stricken U.S.S. Yorktown. He was a ship fitter, and he was using a cutting torch to cut away steel beams that lay over the engine room escape hatch. He had almost cut enough to get the men out. When the word came to abandon ship. He was talking with the engine room crew. There was just enough room to reach his hand through the hatch. So close yet so far. The chief in the engine room asked him to ask the officer next to him for his side arm, and pass it through the opening to him before they left. As they left he could hear the report of the gun. When they left the ship, a destroyer sent a torpedo into the U.S.S. Yorktown. This sailor just couldn't forget this experience, but by talking with him, he was able to get this story off his chest. There is a lot more to this story, and one should read the history on the battle of Midway. In a few days I boarded a troop transport for San Francisco, California. It took a month to cross the ocean, and I landed in Treasure Island, in San Francisco harbor, around the 19th of Jan. 1944. When I went aboard this ship the ships crew assigned the passengers jobs. Some were scrubbing paint, and painting the ship. I was singled out and sent to the engine room. The chief gave me a job of greasing the steering gear, and keeping it clean. The rest of the time was my own.

At the receiving station, instead of eating in the navy mess hall, I went to the ship service chow line. While standing there in the line. I looked up the line and saw my brother Harry, just a few sailors away. I hadn't seen him since January 1942, two years ago. I moved up to him and gave him a punch to his arm, he retaliated by giving me the same. Everybody thought we were fighting. We stopped and told them we were brothers. Harry had been home and was now waiting for a transfer to a diesel school. I told him I was also waiting for, first a 30 day leave and then a diesel school. But first I was going to get married. This was the first he had heard of Vera. As you can see I didn't write too many letters, and neither did he.

We ate dinner together and caught up with each others life again. I received my thirty day leave, and boarded a train for Maine. The train was so crowded, that I had to ride between the coaches. I had a little blue hard backed suit case, that I sat on. The smoke and soot from the steam engine settled on me, and soon I was dirty. By the time we arrived in Cheyenne, Wyoming, or North Platte, Nebraska, I was able to get a seat in the coach. As we neared Chicago, this girl showed up, and she was quite out going. She soon had all of the service men showing her their girl friends picture. She wasn't satisfied with that, and had the pictures circulating around the coach. We entered Chicago about that time and everybody got up and left the train. I never did see Vera's picture again. Some body took it for the picture frame, I guess. It was her high school picture, and I treasured it. It took five days to get to Boston, and then another day to Rockland, Maine. I went straight to Vera's house, as I was afraid, if I went home to Rhode Island, Mom would talk me out of getting married. I know it was the wrong thing to do, but I was determined to get married. I sent Mom a telegram and asked her to come up, and Kinney also. To say the least I wasn't very clean when I got there. Vera's mother took me in. The next day, Vera and I took a taxi, down to the town clerks home. It was a Sunday morning, and we applied for a marriage license. Her name was Eleanor Freddette, and she treated me, Maine style, like she knew me all of her life. She poured me out a cup of coffee, and we filled in the marriage license at her kitchen table. I thought this place was heaven. You can't imagine how I felt. Here was this crummy dirty sailor, who was skinny as a rail, pail and drawn, coming into the Payson house hold and taking their daughter away from them with out any explanation at all. I didn't have enough money to go to a hotel first. I was some lucky to have picked a girl with such a kind and loving family.

Vera and I were married February 6, 1944. We said our marriage vows in the First Baptist church on main street, by Rev. McDonald. As we walked out the door, Vera's relatives and friend threw confetti on us. Then Vera's neighbor Louise Ingraham took us in her car around town blowing her horn, and having a great time. After a while we went to vera's house and had our reception. I met all of the relatives. The nicest people I have ever had the pleasure to meet. Mom and Kenney went home by train that next morning. Vera and I took the bus to Portland that same day, and we spent our first night together in the Eastland Hotel. I remember riding on that bus to Portland and taking side glances at Vera, all the time thinking, what a wonderful girl I had married. Everything had happened so fast, I wondered what her mother was thinking now. Should she have allowed her daughter to get married so quickly, and to some body no body knew or even saw before, except maybe once a year ago. I made up my mind they would never have to worry about her, and some day, maybe I could make them proud of me.

The next day we went on to Pawtucket, Rhode Island. There we met my relatives. What a difference? We returned to Owl's Head, Maine after a few days. Before I knew it, I was on the train going back to San Francisco, Calif. In a couple days I was assigned to the navy's advanced diesel school, Cleveland, Ohio. I got on the train to Boston, Mass. Then I went out to Tewksbury, Mass. and picked up my wife, and left for Cleveland, Ohio. Vera rode the Pullman car and I rode the coach. Neither of us had any idea where she would stay when we got there, in the late afternoon. Through the U.S.O. at the train station, we found a private home in Lakewood. The next day I went into the navy school. During our orientation, one of the instructors there, came up to me and said, "Hi". I didn't recognize him at all. He told me, that on the first troop transport, the SS President Hayes. The transport that took me back to the states in 1942, when I got off the U.S.S. Solace. He had been assigned to watch over me, for my own safety. He said the navy warned him that I had a rough time in the Pacific, and they didn't quite know what I would do, when I got close to the U.S.

He told me to keep my "nose clean," (Navy talk to stay out of trouble, and study hard.") He really didn't have to say that, as I wanted to learn as much as I could. I loved the school, and the opportunity to learn. Best of all, I went home every night to my new wife, and home cooked food. At first I had a hard time with my stomach. When I first came back to the states, and met Harry in the ships service chow line. I ate mashed potato's, roast beef, vegetables, and cake, and a glass of milk. I came down with the hives. It was so bad I had to eat nothing but just plain sandwiches. Now in Cleveland, my stomach was giving me heart burn and stomach aches. I wanted to throw up. I had to go to the Hospital in Great Lakes, Ill. After a few days, I would come home again. I had to learn how to eat all over again, a little at a time.

The six weeks went by quickly, and in the end, I was retained as an instructor. I was to teach the series 71 GM diesel engine. I had to write my own curriculum. This meant, I had to do some research. I read everything I could find at the school. Then found out that I could go out to the industrial plants around Cleveland. I would ride the street car all over Cleveland to these plants. When I arrived, the plant engineer would take me around and show me their manufacturing process. I learned a lot, and gained a good back ground of how the engine was manufactured. I built a good curriculum, with good information for my classes. My first class consisted of twenty nine students. They were made up of Coast Guard and Navy Officers, and some of these officers had just graduated from college. Ail of these students had diesel experience. I didn't try to get them to think that I was some great diesel expert. I told them the truth about me and my diesel experience. We had a good six weeks study. At the end of the course, they said I was able to teach them some very interesting points about that engine. Before they left the school, the training officer had each student write an evaluation on my ability as an instructor. The reports were all very good and the recommendations were excellent. There aren't words in my vocabulary to express my joy.

I just couldn't imagine life could be so good. We moved into a private home, with another sailor and his wife. They were about ten to twelve years older then we were. They had a ten year old daughter, by the name of Beverly. Her mothers name was Gweyn, and her fathers name was Gilbert Bronson. I had to learn how to eat all over again. Gwyen would try different kinds of meals on me. She would get mad at me if I didn't eat all she put on my plate. I tried to force the food down, only to have heart burn. She was a good cook, but after awhile I would have to go to the Great Lakes Naval Hospital for treatment. After a week or two eating that soft food, I would be all right again. I had x-rays and the G.I. series. They couldn't find any thing wrong with me, and they sent me back to the school. I quit smoking. Little by little I got used to eating the richer foods. I had a nerve that wrapped around my stomach like a vise. During those days at sea, I couldn't eat more than a spoon full at a time. On the U.S.S. Hull the Destroyer, I would go into the galley, and take a bowl and help myself to beans and baloney, but only if I was invited to do this by another sailor. I went without a lot of meals because of this. When you have a lot of fear, you don't have much of an appetite. I drank a lot of coffee. I think that was what sustained me during those days at sea. I would put a lot of canned milk in my coffee because the coffee was so strong. On the Battleship U.S.S. Massachusetts, when we went into the Pacific, we ate Chile con Carne every day for six months. That was all we had to eat as we lost most of our food when the storage of potato's spoiled. After we ate the chile up we had Macaroni and Spam for six months, that's the way it was. On the U.S.S. Oklahoma, it wasn't unusual to get fried eggs that were green on the bottom. All in all I ate very little. I had that fear with me for many years after the war was over. I remember during the Korean war I had it all over again. I think what bothered me the most was not being able to see what was going on. I was an engineer, and spent all of my time down below decks. Suspense can amplify your fear. I had a problem with night mares. I would wake up and find all the guy's standing around my bunk staring at me. They were afraid to wake me because they didn't know how I would react. I told them I had a dream I was riding bare naked down a mountain on a bicycle with a mountain lion on my back. Some times I was in the girls toilet naked, or I would be walking down the street in Searsport with Vera holding my hand. I've had these nightmares all my life. Now days I wake up in the night time and I am living through that escape from the USS Oklahoma. Only now I am trying to figure out what to do, what it would be like not to have that hatch cover open. I have to get up and walk around to get my mind out of that track

The threat of war was always there. Every once in a while a name would be placed on our bulletin board. One of our instructors would be transferred at nine o'clock to some ship on the west coast. I was afraid it would happen to me. I would go down to the training officer's office and demand a transfer to the west coast. I wanted enough time to send my family home on the next train. The training officer would calm me down and tell me not to worry, I wouldn't be transferred. When the war was over, Vera had him out to the house for supper. He told us then, that he couldn't have transferred me at any time. He said I had a strong friend in Washington. Who, I have never been able to find out. The only thing I can relate this to, is the chief engineer on the USS Massachusetts. He must have put in a strong recommendation for me to have shore duty. It wasn't until this past year, when I went to see a movie, "Saving Private Ryan." The movie was based on a little known law passed by congress. Any family that had four or more sons in the service, one of them would have to be taken out of front line service and returned back to the states. I can remember my mother calling the Governor of Rhode Island twice at the start of the war. Asking if her sons had survived the attack on Pearl Harbor. Then again she called the governor and wanted to know why I wasn't paid, she told him I had not been paid for six months. I can remember that time, I was in New York in pier 92 receiving station, and standing in the pay line waiting to see the pay master. But every day his office would close before I could ever get there. I suppose that my name was fresh on somebody's mind in Washington. I really don't think that my sea duty would have had that much effect, I don't know .I remember my division officer had asked me how much sea duty I had. I told him I had thirty nine months, with out hesitation. That's one thing we all kept track of.

We had our baby in January, 1945, at about the same time we moved to a small house next door, to where we were staying. We bought the furniture in the house for five hundred dollars, all the money we had in our savings account. The man that owned the house next door was an electrical engineer. (Ed Kopas). He would help me with my studies on Electricity. I had been studying the text book, Elements of Electricity when I first went on board the USS Massachusetts. The diesel school was located next to the General Motors factory, that was building the Model 278-A and the 268-A GM diesel engines. The 268-A's were generating units. I found that I needed the back ground in Electricity.

The other sailor that lived with us, (Gilbert Bronson) had been on the USS Chicago, when she was torpedoed off Savo Island in the fall of 1942. In civilian life he was a garage man. Well we found a car to buy cheap. It was a 1929 Jordan. We over hauled the engine. In the process Vera was very jealous of that car. I had a hard time trying to figure that out. One Sunday morning we decided to make a trip over to East Cleveland. We had saved up our Gas Ration stamps all month, or maybe I should say three months. The time it took to over haul the engine. We made the trip and burned up all of our gas in one trip. Another time we saved up our gas stamps for three months, and then made a trip to a friends house in Akron, Ohio. We got to our friends house. On the way home we were running out of gas. It was late and Vera was afraid the baby would run out of milk. Gilbert went into a fire station and asked the firemen if they would sell us some gas. They said they couldn't sell us any gas, but they would give us some.

One of the reasons, I became concerned about the time I had left at the school. I was running out of students. I would go two or three weeks without a class. I remember one afternoon in my class room. A thunder storm came through. I stood at the window and marveled at the beauty of the rain. I had a hard time adjusting to such an easy way of life. I spent a lot of time in the GM diesel plant. I wanted to learn as much as I could about these engines. I also wanted to be busy, time went faster that way.

One Saturday morning, we were standing captains inspection. We were lined up along the side walks in front of our barracks. The Captain stepped forward and made an announcement. President Roosevelt had died. We were all at a loss as to what we would do now. It wasn't long and, we were at captains inspection again. The captain announced, the war with Germany was over. Then four months later we were lined up for captains inspection.

The captain stepped forward and made an announcement. The United States Air Force had dropped an Atomic Bomb on Japan. We didn't know what an Atomic bomb was, but we could feel that it was a terrible thing. Everybody was stock still. I think we were all in shock. Then one man fainted and fell with an awful sound onto the pavement. I felt that we were entering into a whole new era, and a time of a new kind of fear.

The advent of the Atomic bomb brought about the end of the war with Japan. Now I was occupied with closing down the school. I had to inventory all of my tool's, and spare parts, etc. The engines all twenty eight of them had to be crated, and shipped to a rehabilitation hospital, in California. During this time, we were having a great time with parties. At first in some body's private home. Then we moved up town to the hotels. We were spending the ship service money, which had accumulated during the war. Harry and Kinney got out of the Navy early, and they came out to visit Vera and I. Life was some good, we enjoyed each other, and had a great time. I couldn't remember ever being so happy. Finally I was transferred to the Great Lakes Naval Training Station. The instructors were to set up the new post war advanced diesel school. We had every diesel engine the navy used in service. I had the Cooper Bessemer diesel engine to write a curriculum for. I was nearing the end of my enlistment. The school training officer called me into his office one day and offered me Chief Motor Machinist mate, if I would ship over for, four more years. This was a great plum for me. However it made me very mad. After all this time in the navy. Now they were going to give me Chief Petty officer. I couldn't afford the change in uniform, and I didn't intend to ship over I turned the offer down. I was afraid that if I shipped over my marriage would not last. I was a father now and I wouldn't let anything interfere, with raising my son.

When I entered the Naval Separation center, there was only three sailors getting their discharge. All that was left of a hundred men from my company, I thought. Just a few years ago I received a Pearl Harbor Survivors magazine. It had a company picture of Co. 37-40. This was my boot camp picture, I remember when they took it but didn't have one. I wrote the man that had sent it in, and he said there was a mix up when he was discharged and he had to wait until the next day for his discharge.

Family Life

I remember standing out side of the Naval training station and slowly getting used to the idea that I was on my own. I didn't have to go back. I was free. At first I felt a little timid. Now I couldn't fool around, I had to get to my next home and get a job. I took the train to Cleveland, and have my tools, that were stored at Ed Kopas house shipped home to Rockland, Maine. These were the tools, that were given to me from the Cleveland Naval Diesel school. When the war was over, we closed the school down. The training officer asked me to make up a set of tool's for him, me, and the Captain, of the base. I also had a clothes washer, and a Divan, left over from a house full of furniture, that we had, when we were living in Cleveland. I also had a one cylinder series "71" diesel generator set, and an assortment of spare parts. I shipped all of this home by freight car, (train).

When I received my Honorable Discharge from the Navy, I also received one hundred dollars mustering out pay, and also $19.40 travel allowance, and $72.66 of my earned pay. I was told I would get $100.00 a month for the next two months to get me started on my own. I was also supposed to get $20.00 a week for one year, or until I got a job. I received one check for $20.00. The state unemployment office gave me such a hard time about those checks, I told them to shove their money up their *#~. We had to live with Vera's parents until I could get a job. Everybody I talked to, wanted to know if I had any experience. I would tell them about my navy training. It never seemed to satisfy them. Nobody wanted to pay anything, or they weren't hiring. You had to grow up in Rockland to get a job. Vera's father got me a job, helping a farmer get his hay into the barn. One days work for two bucks. I soon got tired of giving my life history. Then with out those employment requests from the employer, the state denied payment. My legs were giving me a lot of pain, and I was worried, if I got a job, how could I keep it, if I had to walk to work, then walk home afterward. I had several veins in my legs that had worked out to the skin, and my pants were rubbing on them and they were bleeding and causing the pain. I went to a doctor, and he asked me how much money I had? I told him I had one $100.00 coming to me from the government, next month. He said he would set up the operation, and do the job for the $100.00.

My next door neighbor knew I needed a job, and also knew of my knowledge of diesel engines. He gave my name to the manager of the Gulf Oil Co. in Rockland. They needed a relief engineer on the Rockland Gulf oil tanker. They hired me for two weeks vacation, at good pay. That was in August 1946. This same neighbor, (Dan Cushman) worked for Standard Oil Co. of New York. He brought me an application form and a good recommendation, using my brief example with the Gulf Oil Corp. as Chief engineer, on the Gulf Oil Tanker. I received the attention of Mr. L.W. Gustafson Division Operating Manager. Standard oil Company of New York. The oil company hired me three months later, the 10th of Dec. 1946. In the mean time, I went down to the A. C. Mcloon Lobster Co. It was a Saturday afternoon. I talked to A. C. McLoon the company owner for over four hours.

I had to tell him my life story, and all of my naval experiences. I got the job as a cook on his lobster smack. $29.00 a week seven days and twenty four hours a day. I worked for him until Dec. 8th.

Then I moved next door and my rent was $45.00 a month. On twenty nine dollars a week, we weren't making it. McLoon assigned me to the Smack "Pauline". She was a wet smack. That is the hold (storage area) had holes bored through her hull. That allowed water to circulate through the hold. As we carried around four thousand lb. of lobsters, for a normal load. We would buy these lobsters from dealers in the out lying islands, up and down the coast. One time we carried around six thousand lb. of lobsters from Matinicus Island, down to Jonesport, Maine, to a lobster pound. We ran all day, first from Rockland, to Matinicus Island. Then down the bay by Isle Au Haut, through Stonington, by Swans Island, across Blue hill Bay, by the Bass Harbor buoy, by Mount Desert Island, on the inside of Great Cranberry Island, Across French mans bay, to Scoodic Island. We became fog bound. We managed to find the island, but not the Scoodic Island bell. Rather than waste too much time looking for the bell, we started out for Moultin's ledge. We ran for about twenty minutes, and decided to change course, and run for Prospect Harbor. I stood up on the bow to watch for shallow water. It was coming on dark and it was scary. You couldn't see twenty feet ahead. I soon spotted a ledge, "The Old Man". We came about just in time. I could have stepped ashore onto that ledge. The wash from the sea kept us from grounding out on that ledge. The ledge looked like a man's bald head. We ran by two more ledges, and then ran right through the anchorage in Prospect harbor in thick of fog, and it was also pitch black. We didn't see a thing. The next morning, we found, we had come through at least eight or ten boats in the anchorage. We had anchored in the only place in the harbor that was available. The fog lifted later in the day, and we continued on to Jonesport that night. We unloaded our lobsters, and found we had lost about a third of our load. We boiled most of them, and after they were cooked, we could tell if they were eatable by flicking their tail. If the tail sprang back it was considered good to eat. At that time our only means of navigation was our compass and our ships clock. The captain had a note book with some courses he had taken when the sky was clear. Most of our navigation was by dead reckoning. On the way home it was still foggy. We went aground on a shoal near Stonington. We managed to get clear after the tide came in later that day, as we entered Stonington the sky cleared, and we made it into Rockland, Sunday afternoon. I took what food there was left in the galley home, as I wouldn't get paid until Monday or Tuesday, if we were in port. That fall my family lived on Deer meat, that Vera's father had shot during hunting season. As the weather got colder, Vera took my navy uniform and made me a shirt I could wear. My navy clothes were worn out that winter.

Monday morning the Pauline was hauled out on A. C. McCloon's marine railway for repairs, as the ledge had weakened her keel. I removed the engines reduction gear and replaced the oil seal, which had been leaking. During this time we had to make a trip out to Matinicus Island. We had to take an old smack, "the Mary Ann" she was an old condemned lobster smack. We made Matinicus Island O.K., loaded our lobsters. We left the Island around 12 noon for Rockland. Normally a four hour trip, (Matinicus Island is only 18 miles from Rockland). A north west breeze came up, and as those sea's hit us, her old timbers began to creak, and she started to take on water. The old gas engine quit. I had to man the bilge pump, a hand operated pump on deck. The captain would get that engine to run for a few minutes at a time. We made Rockland harbor around nine o'clock that night. My brother Kenney met us at the dock and helped us unload. Then he told me the man from standard oil had called to tell me I had the job, and to report for work Monday morning Dec. 10, 1946.

I had never driven a truck before. The guys I worked with were the best. They taught me how to drive a truck, and how to back it up. I loved every minute of it. My job was to deliver Kerosene to the houses around the area. My first trip, I delivered in the town of Warren. Bernard "Bum" Robinson showed me where to go and the names of the people. Two weeks later they sent me out alone, and expected me to remember where to go and the names of these people, also where they hid the key to their house and their credit rating. Mean while I had made some twelve other trips, from Rockland to Liberty, to Searsport and Stockton Springs delivering oil to houses all over the place. Some of the time seven and eight o'clock at night. It wasn't easy, and I had to go in the houses and ask what their names were. I could remember the house and the locations. Almost every women I met had to know who I was and where I came from. I had to relate my life story, and some of my navy experiences. How I met Vera etc. This way I gained their confidence, and trust. Which was important, as they had to trust me with the key to their house. Usually the key was hid outside on the house some where. I had one trip to Liberty, Maine. It was about thirty miles from Rockland, and up a mountain. My truck could hardly make it up over the top. I carried one thousand gallons of kerosene, and sold all of it in that one town. I got to know almost everybody in this area of Maine. The first week I worked some eighty hours, and with the time and a half for over time, my first pay check was $111.00. I worked three months before I found out that I had a day off. It came on a Tuesday. This was a good job. I found out, I had two weeks vacation every year, plus ten paid holidays. To me this was unheard of. I also had hospital insurance. Vera gave birth to James my second son in Sept. 1947, and the insurance paid every cent of the hospital costs. One of the conditions of my employment. I had to go to Portland and the Marine inspectors office, and apply for a Chief Engineer's license, in the U.S. Merchant Marine. Based on my Naval training, and a tough written exam, and a tough first aid exam, I was able to get this license. I kept it for thirty years. Working for the Standard Oil Co. who changed their name to Socony Vacuum, then Socony, then to the Mobil Oil Corp. I used my license to go as relief engineer on the Mobil Oil Tanker Cape Ann Socony. We traveled the length of the Maine Coast, from Cape Elizabeth to Machias, down East. I preferred to stay on the land and drive truck, although the pay was higher on the tanker. I didn't like the tanker job, because, We would load on a Monday morning and go down east to Jonseport and unload, then come back to Hancock reload, and deliver this load on the way back to Rockland. Arriving on a Sunday afternoon. When I first went on this tanker, our only means of navigation was our compass, clock, and listening for a navigational bell or whistle buoy, I spent many a cold day on the bow of this tanker listening for these buoys.

In the spring of 1948, the oil company gave us an increase cost of living allowance. Mine came to around $80.00. I borrowed two hundred dollars from Vera's sister Eleanor. I was looking for a house to buy. I always went toward Rockland to look for a house. I came home from work one afternoon, and Vera said I found some land to buy down in Owl's Head, lets go and see the land owner, and look at the land. We went up over Ingrahams Hill and down over the other side. To the Ralph Everret farm.

The land we were to buy was across the road. Ralph Everret showed us some land in the field. It was across and down the field one lot below ours. I thought this land was too wet, and decided not to buy. Ralph, not wanting to loose the sale, suggested I buy the first lot in the field. I thought the lot was too small. So he suggested I buy two lots. Each lot was $125.00. I bought two lots, one below the other, for $250. It was about 45 ft on the road, 217 ft down towards the shore, and 58 ft across the bottom. I paid cash for them. The closing costs were one dollar. It was the first house in the field to be built.

I used to go over to Vera's father's shop in the evening after work. I asked Harry if he would help me build my house. Harry, suggested I go up country and buy an old cow barn. A barn with the boards nailed up and down. I went up country to Searsmont, and bought an old hay barn. I paid $80.00 for it. I didn't know it then, but it was made out of Hemlock boards. Harry meant for me to buy a barn made from pine boards. I took the barn down in eight days, and hauled all of it down to my lot, in the eight days. I had a 1931 Buick model 90. A big eight cylinder car, with a home made trailer. Some of the planks and timbers were thirty feet long. I laid these long timbers on the trailer and then used the other end to tie to my car bumper. I hauled all of my lumber from the barn home, and had it done by the end of August 1948. At first I made a two foot square frame, about a foot deep. I filled them with cement all twelve of them. This barn had a lot of big beams, 6x6's, and 4x4'.

I used the 6x6's and stood them up, about three feet, and used the 4x4's for braces. I mounted the bottom frame work of my house on top of these 6x6's. I had numbered all of the 2x6's from the barn, so now all I had to do was put them together, the same way they came apart from the barn. All of the floor joists were mortised and tenon. I nailed the boards on. Then had Harry come down and help me put the studs up. I was able to buy all of my studs from Ed Wotton, (one of Vera's friends).

I hired Harry to work on the house, as I had to work. I worked evenings and weekends. Harry worked for $.50 an hour, the going rate for carpenters those days was $1.00 an hour. At the same time I started to dig the trench for my city water pipe. It had to be five feet deep, and we measured every inch of it. When I got down to the corner of the house I ran into a ledge. After some very hard digging with a pick ax, I managed to work my way around the ledge without going under the house. I placed boards over the top of the pipe line, and covered the trench up, all seventy feet of it. Next came the job of building my chimney. I found some second hand brick up in Lincolnville beach, I bought them for around $.03 each. I figured out how many bricks I would need per foot then estimated the height. I started to build the chimney. Then I had to go engineer on the Cape Ann Socony. I was gone two weeks, and when I returned winter had set in and I had to wait for spring and warmer weather. Around the first of April, we started in again. Harry was working on the kitchen cupboards, and I worked on the chimney. I had the water into the house and a kitchen sink. That's all. The week before Memorial Day I moved all of our furnishings into the house. Then left for a weeks vacation up to Moosehead Lake fishing. Harry, Albert, (Vera's brother), Owen Allen, and me.

We were gone three days and we were back. I went to work on my cement foundation. All spring I had been going over to Cushing, (Fale's Gravel pit) I had a 1934 Pick-up truck and a home made trailer. I bought this 1934 Chevrolet truck for $200.00. The first thing I did was over haul the engine, (new rings, bearings and a valve job.) Then rebuild the front end, (new king pins). Then make a rear fender, out of a piece of tin I had. After work I would go over to Cushing and load my truck and trailer. I would jack knife the trailer. Then when it came time to leave, I would start and go around in a circle until I had built up enough speed to get me up out of that gravel pit. As I came up over the top of the pit, my engine would be just barely turning over. If any one of those six cylinders misfired, I would have been stranded. I would get home just in time for supper. The next night I would go over to, what is now the Rockland city dump, (A lime rock quarry) and load up with lime rock. I had a big pile of sand and lime rock in front of my house near the road. I started to dig at the rear of the house and dug just one end. Then made a set of cement forms that reached across the rear of the house, just four feet high, half the height I needed to go. I poured my first cement on Memorial Day 1949. To do this I had to borrow Gordan Simmon's cement mixer. First I had to repair the motor and cord, and clean out the old dry cement in it. No easy job. Then I used a wash tub and two five gallon buckets, a brush, and a big trowel. I used the brush to scrub clean every lime stone put into the cement. I put as many stones in the cement as I could. This conserved cement. At the end of the wall, I made the cement thick, that way the cement wouldn't run out of the end of my forms. I finished the foundation on Oct. 13 1949. My foundation was 20'x30' by 6' high. I paid $90.00 for cement at $.90 a bag, and $5.00 or 6.00 for the sand. The lime rock was free.

At this time the Korean War was starting up, actually the threat of war with Korea was heating up, during 1947. I remember being afraid of being called back into service. I was a diesel engine expert, and that meant I would be on a landing craft, or mine sweeper. I was experiencing the fear pains in my stomach again. Maybe I should explain, (fear pains) I had a nerve that wrapped itself around my stomach like a vise, also I had a lot of gas pain that I couldn't let out. It came up as a burp. I had a lot of indigestion. As time went by I learned to talk about these fears and was able to live with them. I started to relate my experience to my church Sunday School Class, Fifty years later and I'm still doing it. As the years went by I had to learn to live with these awful times. How many times I would wake up during the night thinking about those days. The worst times were in the fall months, during November and December. I noticed that once Dec. 7 had passed, my fears subsided. I guess you could call nightmares.

A lot of times when I got through work and I was late as I had worked over time. My friend Bill Butman who was my next door neighbor, would come to his kitchen window and wave a coffee pot. That was a signal to come over for his wife's famous venison pie. That started us getting together for a party. Vera picked my birthday, which was Dec. 19. From that time on we had a birthday party for me. Later it was expanded to include about five or six friends who had birthdays during Dec.

That brings me to remember a time years ago. It was thanksgiving and Harry and I were invited to a thanksgiving dinner with some people from our church. I remember sitting at this table with a turkey and all the fixings. I had eaten all I could and, was thinking about Everett and Kenney and Mom. I reached out and took a leg from the turkey and pit it in my pocket. The lady caught me in the act. She wanted to know what I did that for. I told her, I took it for my brothers at home. She had me put it back and she would fix up a dinner for Mom, Kenney and Everett.

That fall, I had been filling in on the Cape Ann Socony as their Chief Engineer. It was on one of these trips on the Cape Ann. We had spent the week down East to Beals Island, (Jonesport) It was a Saturday afternoon. As we came up to Monroes Island bell. I picked up our binoculars to look for my house. I saw, what appeared to be, some Chinese junks. I don't know what brought that on, as I had never seen a Chinese junk before. (They were fishing boats from Germany.) Their name's were, the Squall, Surge, and the Wave. I think there were six or seven of these boats. That was odd, I thought, then I took another look at Rockland harbor. Then it came to me. Long ago, when the war first started, and I was on the U.S.S. Hull DD 350. I used to pray every night before going to sleep. I said a simple prayer, Now I lay me down to sleep etc. Then I would continue on with thinking about some future day when I was out of the Navy and the war would be over.

I visualized in my mind, a girl, I would some day marry. I remember a thought coming to my mind. What does she look like? I couldn't think of anybody I could name. But I could remember a picture of a girl on a package of needles my mother had. It seemed to me that I was actually talking with God. At the time I felt that I was being pushed into naming a certain person, I couldn't do that, as I had never had a real girl friend. Next I would visualize my home, that I would build on the shore of a great body of water. The only difference, here, my house was on salt water. Out in the Pacific I thought I was talking about fresh water, but I didn't specify fresh water. Now looking at this place from the water I could see my prayer come true. I just couldn't believe it at first, I looked again, and a shiver went down my back, I also had to hide a tear. I thought, GOD had not only granted my prayer, but now, God wanted me to see it come true. I didn't let captain Ray Cousins know anything about this, he just kept on steering the vessel in to port.

Harry Payson was building my kitchen cabinets. He was using the best boards we had bought, when I received my first loan from the bank. This is interesting. When I went to the Rockland Savings and loan to borrow some money ($500.00) so I could buy the materials I needed, they wanted to know if I had any collateral. I told them, I had started to build my house. They turned me down, as I didn't have a cement foundation. Harry had to talk to his brother-in-law, Audrey Orff to get the loan approved. Audrey was on the board of directors for the bank. We had gone over to Overlocks lumber yard in Warren, and he picked over a whole pile of lumber, picking out the best boards. Harry knew just what he needed for lumber. He was picking out the house trim boards, also the boards for my window frames and door frames, and the boards he would use to build my kitchen cabinets. Everything in the house was home made. I bought the window sash, and made the window frames. Harry had an old front door, and we made the door frame. I also bought the kitchen door with a window in it for three dollars. I finished my chimney, in April 1949. Harry had the kitchen done that May. I hauled Harry's old chicken coop down to my house, and I made an out house out of it. We moved in the day before Memorial Day. The only room in the house that was finished was the kitchen. I left everything on the floor, and went fishing.

We went up above Moosehead Lake, then another 35 miles to Seboomook Dam. That first night we slept in this old building. We later learned the barn was the barracks for WW 11 prisoners from Germany. The first day we were there, the dam was shut down, and we were able to catch our limit of trout, and salmon. That afternoon, the dam was opened, and our fishing went with it. After the third day we left for home.

It was Memorial Day and I started to pour cement for my foundation. I would pour cement on the week ends and dig the trench during the week nights after work. I used those big 6x6 thirty foot long timbers across the ends of the house to hold the house up. Later I would use these holes for my cellar windows. Actually I made the window frames out of two inch planks that I had, and installed them before the cellar wall cement was poured. That way the cement bonded to the window. At the same time I was doing this, I was shingling the house, when time permitted.

Around the middle of June, I was digging the trench on the north side of the house, and I run into a big rock. It was exactly under the sill. It was about six feet in diameter. I couldn't move it. I asked Harry, what I could do about it. He said, bury it. I did just that. I dug a hole just outside of my wall, and went down about ten feet and ten feet wide. Then I poured some water on the clay, and with a pry bar, I slid the rock into the hole. A lot of work. I dug the trench during the week days after work. I dug the trench just wide enough for the cellar wall plus enough room for the forms, then I would brace the forms with boards and braces driven into the ground out side. If I run out of sand and rock, I would go after sand or rock after work at 4:00 PM.

I could be home for supper at 6 o'clock. Then I would dig until dark. I finished the cellar wall on Columbus day in October 1949. I left the cellar roll away open at the end. When winter set in I insulated inside and put up sheet rock. I bought enough sheet rock from Vic Johnson, for $45.00 to sheet rock the whole house up and down. I was putting up sheet rock standing on my bed in the living room. I made my saw table out of an arbor, that I had from my tools from the U.S. Navy. The electric motor came from an old junked gasoline pump. I bought a four inch jointer, and a orbital sander. With these tools I finished the inside work. That winter during the January thaw, Albert Payson and I dug the rest of the dirt out from under the house. We used Harry's wheel barrow, and put the dirt out on the front lawn. That February I started to lay down my living room floor. Vera took Jimmy and Johnny by train to Tewksbury, Mass. (Ella Bernssons house) for a visit. I put the grain of the wood together in such a way as to make the floor very attractive.

James was my second child, he was born Sept. 26, 1947. We named him James Everett. In honor of my brother Everett, Who was living in White Bear Lake, Minnesota. Everett was the one who had to leave home when he was thirteen years old and had grown up on the farm in Grove City, Minnesota. Jimmy was a cute little boy. I remember taking him home and wondering what his personality would be like. He cried a lot, and was lovable and cuddly.

I had a 1931 Buick model #90, a big passenger car, with a luggage rack on the rear bumper. On a Friday after work, we would load the two kids in the back seat with pillows and a blanket, and a light lunch. We headed out for Pawtucket, Rhode

Island, to visit my mother, and two brothers. (Harry and Kinney) I carried a five gallon can of gas, and a five gallon can of oil. The oil company had allowed me to clean out five 2000 gallon lube oil tanks. These tanks were put to use, on the Islands for fuel oil storage. The price of gas was around 25¢ a gallon, and the trip down was around 200 miles. The Maine turn pike was 45 miles long then from Portland to Portsmouth, N.H. I drove my car 45 miles an hour. I was afraid the motor couldn't stand a higher speed, Also I got better gas mileage that way. Sunday morning Kinney would drive my car around the block until the bar rooms would open, so he could have a drink. Kinney loved to drive. His main ambition was to drive a truck. After a while Kinney would drive down here to Maine and stay with me. Court Eleanor, Vera's sister. Kinney married Eleanor, and they moved to Rhode Island.

The state of Minnesota was giving its veterans a $400.00 bonus. My brother Everett helped me file an application for it. With this money I bought, a Model FQ 90 Lenox hot air furnace, a bath tub, a toilet, bath room lavatory, a 20 foot length of 3" copper pipe, a 275 gallon oil tank, with an oil gauge, and automatic shut off valve. Ail for $400.00. That was in March of 1953.

On February 20 1953, our third child was born. Nancy Lou, she was named after me, because I wanted a girl for such a long time. Vera said she wanted a new refrigerator, and a television set. Television was just coming into Maine at that time. I started on the septic system. After reading up on septic tanks and leach fields. I started in and dug the hole for my septic tank. I made my tank out of cement. I used the left over forms from my cellar foundation. Cutting them down to size. I figured a 500 gallon tank would be big enough. For a leach field, I dug a trench three feet deep, and about A hundred feet long, down the side of my lot. Then used perforated 0rangebird fiber pipe. This pipe lasted about thirty five years. Then in 1988, I dug it all up and installed a trench Three foot deep and three wide, then I laid a foot of rock. Then I connected my four inch perforated plastic pipe on top of the rock. Then I made from ten inch by two inch pressure treated planks a "V" shaped cover over the pipe. I cut notches in the planks to allow the fluid to drain out. Then I covered this over with a foot of rock, and the balance with dirt. I have a system now that goes down the middle of my back yard. The only evidence that shows where the leach field is located. In the summer if it is dry, the lawn turns brown. I installed the plumbing in the house. The three inch piece of copper pipe, was just long enough to run from the cellar to the second floor, with a short jog over to the side of the bath room, then up through the roof. We had our inside toilet by the end of April 1953. The furnace came in small pieces, and I had to put it together. The first thing I did was to make a base for the furnace to set on. Then put the furnace together. The combustion chamber was the hardest. The fire brick didn't fit as I had put cement between the edges of the brick. I had to cut away some of the brick, to get it in. Years later this part of the fire brick caused trouble. I should never have used any cement between the brick. I got the duck pipe in, and the furnace wired, and ready to go on Oct. 13, 1953. When a boil formed on my neck. I went to the Doctor's office, and Doctor North, put a shot of Penicillin into the middle of the boil. That afternoon, my ankles began to swell. I went home sick. That night I began to swell up all over, and itch. Vera was covering me with baking soda. In the morning, Vera called Dr. Lawry, and he came out to see me around noon. He took one look at my throat, and said it was a God send. He had received these pills that very morning. Then he told me I was allergic to Penicillin. The swelling started to go down that afternoon. I had two red lines on my skin, one starting at my temples and going down my neck to my belly button. The other line started on my legs and went up to my belly button. It took a week before I could walk. The soles of my feet felt as though they had been skinned. The weather turned cold, and I had to call a friend in to start my furnace.

I remember buying six or seven gallons of paint from the oil company. Six gallons of white and one gallon of green, for trim. I wasn't looking forward to painting the house, when some guys from Massachusetts were painting the oil tanks at the plant. They agreed to paint my house, and charged me $16.00 for two coats, and they did it one evening after work. They had an air compressor and sprayed the paint on. It was a good job well done. One thing that made all of this work worth while. When Vacation time came around, we dropped everything and piled into the car, and went either camping, or visiting my brother out in Minnesota. In 1958 Harry took his car and I took my 1955 Ford station wagon. Our first night we spent in a farmer's field. We cooked our breakfast on my camp stove right in the field next to the car. In Minnesota we visited my old friend Gray Jordan, and the Ovals out in Grove City. Coming home we drove to Niagara Falls, and there we went to sleep. A policeman woke us up and told us to move. I told him I was too tired. Every year we went camping up north usually Moosehead Lake. During these years I worked the late shift, so I had the mornings off. I would work on the house until around nine thirty then take Nancy and go up town to Newberts restaurant and have a cup of coffee and a donut, and Nancy would have a dish of ice cream. One night when Nancy was a baby, she woke up and began to cry around 2 o'clock in the morning. Vera pregnant with Ann and was too tired to get up to feed her. So I did, and after I got her to sleep again, I stayed up and drove up to Bingham, Maine, and the Wyman Dam. I stood on the shore next to the dam and caught five or six Salmon.

Ann Marie born fifteen months after Nancy. She was a cute little girl, and between the two of them, Vera had her hands full. I worked the afternoon and evening shift. When I came home, Nancy would be crying. I would pick her up and in a few minutes she would be asleep in my arms. Each spring I took my vacation, a week in June, and made my annual trip to Moosehead Lake, fishing. We slept in my lean-to tent, and fished from my home made boat. One year we climbed Spencer Mountain, and another time I took Nancy and Ann on a trip to Lobster Lake. This was a great adventure in the Maine wilderness for us. I had never been to Lobster Lake before. I had to go north of Moosehead lake, to North East Carry, go down to the West branch of the Penobscot river. Launch my boat, and leave my car in the field. Then go down the river five or six miles, then pick a likely looking stream, and go another five or six miles, to get into Lobster lake. It sounds easy, but I had never been there before, and had to guess as to where we were. We crossed the lake and looked for a camp ground for the night. This being the Fourth of July weekend, the few camp sites that were there were all taken up by other campers. Well we squeezed in, I pitched my tent. Then we went out fishing. The wind started to blow, and we had to come in. My tent was blown right out straight by the wind. I had to take the tent down and put it up some where else. I picked a big Cedar tree, near the camp ground and near the water. I opened up the lower part of the tree, and then pitched my tent under the great big branches. That evening it started to thunder and rain. We got into the tent and never heard another thing until morning. It rained hard that night and you could see where the water ran down beside the tent. We were as snug as a bug in the rug. I made it a point to take my kids on a camping trip alone, when they were around twelve or thirteen years old. As I knew, the years that followed, they would want to go by themselves.

Then in February, 1960, Vera picked up an American Legion magazine and noticed the U.S.S. Oklahoma was having a ships reunion. She wrote to them and inquired about it. We didn't hear anything until April. A newspaper reporter from Oklahoma City wanted Harry and me to come out there to help dedicate a memorial to the U.S.S. Oklahoma. We wrote back, that we couldn't do that as we had families to support and a job to keep. One thing led to another. Then Eleanor Fredette, (the Owl's Head town clerk) got wind of it. She got in touch with Senator Marguerite Chase Smith. About that time, the north Vietnamese started to move into South Vietnam, also the cold war was in full swing. We were trying to contain Communism.

Then a U-2 spy plane was shot down over Russia. Then President Dwight Eisenhower got involved, as Senator Smith read my account of Pearl Harbor to the Armed Services Committee. By recognizing the Pearl Harbor survivors, he had an excuse for the U-2 Plane. It seemed very hush hush to me, as I would be getting these telegrams in the evening, telling me to be ready at a certain time, and be at the Augusta Airport, when they wanted Harry and I. We left one evening around 4 PM. I thought it was strange, there was a small group of people at the airport, (my boss, Mr. Gustafson, from Portland,) Irvin Curtis, and Eleanor Freddette from Owl's Head. Irvin was from the American Legion. That's all I can remember. We boarded the Air National Guard plane and took off. We circled over the Augusta airport for almost an hour, maybe longer. Finally I got up and went in to see the General. I thought that we wouldn't arrive in Washington in time to board the Admiral's air plane. I was sure he wasn't going to wait for me. General Hayward told me President Eisenhower wanted Harry and me on that plane, and Admiral Arleigh Burke would wait for us in Washington, before flying out to Oklahoma city. We boarded the Secretary of the Navy's Airplane. Then Admiral Arliegh Burke, Chief of Naval Operations joined us, and we took off for Oklahoma City. The Admiral had two aides with him, a Navy Captain and a Marine Colonel, and the Admirals Wife. A pretty navy Wave brought all of us a cocktail. We settled down to a long rough flight through some thunder and lightning storms. The Admiral came back and sat with us, and we talked about our war time experiences. He told me at that time that the torpedo's that hit the Oklahoma were of a special design. They were supposed to have had a double war head on them, and that explained the double explosion we experienced. Fifty years later we learned that was wrong. We were hit by nine torpedos, with conventional war heads, with special wooden fins bolted on the rear of the torpedo. The admiral and his wife were very nice to us. He read his speech to us, the one he would give tomorrow at the Chamber of Commerce luncheon in Oklahoma city. It was a major U.S. foreign policy speech aimed at North Vietnam. North Vietnam was beginning to invade south Vietnam, and also to inform Russia that the U.S. didn't forget the attack on Pearl Harbor on 7 December 1941. We were there to reinforce that policy. I remember having to stand up with the other guy's there, every time the admiral mentioned our names. There were four of us from around the country, and one man from Oklahoma city. The Chamber of Commerce served us dinner. I had a steak dinner, and was too excited to eat. Bob Kinderman came by train from Oshkosh, WI. That first morning we went down to the capital and met the newspaper girl that wrote to me that spring, together we went to see the governor of Oklahoma in his office. We had brought a State of Maine gift package to be given to him from the governor of the State of Maine. In return the Governor of the State of Oklahoma made all of us honorary Colonels of the state of Oklahoma. After the Chamber of Commerce luncheon, we left by motor car, and at sixty miles an hour through town with sirens going we boarded our plane for Ponca City, Oklahoma. I invited Bob to come along with us. When the admiral came aboard I introduced Bob to him with an explanation, about his war experience. Bob rode with us up to Ponca City, 0klahoma. There was a very exclusive girls college. They were having a graduation ceremony, and we were required to sit up on the stage with admiral Burke, while he gave his speech.

  I remember the suit I wore was only about five years old. When I arrived that evening my pants split down the middle. Luckily I had brought along a spare pair of pants, and a sport jacket, which I put on, but no tie. Now up here in Ponca City, that afternoon they took us out to a very exclusive country club. Everybody was dressed in suits and very formal. They all looked down their noses at me. I tried to explain what had happened, and I didn't have a spare tie. That evening, we had supper at this teachers house, and he loaned me a tie for that evening's commencement ceremony. The admiral again gave a U.S. policy speech. I guess these speeches were designed to ease the S.E.A.T.O. (South East Asia Treaty Organization) countries worries over North Vietnam.

  When Harry and I got home, I took off for Moosehead Lake, and camped out on a remote Island with my boat and tent for a few days, to get my courage back to face the newspaper people. Later that summer we met the pilot of the air national guard plane, and his family at Moosehead lake. We shared a Salmon or two with them, and later they visited our home in Owl's Head.

  All during this time, from Dec. 10, 1946, to October 1961, I was doing everything I could to be able to take any of the several jobs in the plant, as a vacation relief. I obtained a Chief Engineers License, and a Captain's license to operate passenger carrying vessels. I did this so as to operate the Cape Ann Socony, our tanker that supplied the islands along the coast of Maine. These were U.S. Coast Guard licenses. I also took two years of advanced business courses. These were night classes.

As I was on the bottom of the seniority list, I had to work the afternoon shift (1/30 to 9/30 PM). There wasn't that much work for the afternoon shift, and I found I had plenty of time to do other kinds of work to keep busy. At first I washed the trucks,& Greased them, then I washed the office, sanded the work counter and finished the counter with a coat of varnish. Then I painted the office. Now I was running out of work. Every once in awhile I had a chance to fill in as the Yard man. This job required the skill to measure the product in the storage tanks. Those storage tanks were thirty five feet high. You had to know the height of the product in each tank in order to measure it. To do that I would add up the total Gallons sold, then subtract those gallons from the last measurement. From there I had an idea where to look on the tape for this measurement. The steel measuring tape was all steel, you could find the liquid level by turning the tape around to the back side. Then turn the tape around to get the exact measurement. Some of the time it took several tries, to arrive at the exact measurement especially the gasoline's. Fuel Oil was easy but gasoline was very hard, as it would evaporate when the tape was lifted up into the air. This was a very cold job, as my hands were covered with gasoline or fuel oil, and with the wind blowing, the wind chill factor it was very cold. The same with loading my truck in the winter time. My gloves were soaked with oil, and it was hard to keep my hands warm. To keep them from freezing, I would open and close them rapidly to get the blood flowing. At the end of the month, we would measure the tanks and take a sample of the product from each tank. We tested the gasoline's with a hydrometer, and use a closed cup for a flash temperature. Kerosene had a flash point of 120°F, and Fuel Oil was 165° and Diesel oil was 185° as I remember. Usually, we had a Barge (Boston Fuel Co.) come to our dock and fill our tanks. It would take about eight hours to unload, either at night or all day. When the barge left our dock we would have to go down and drain into our trucks about 500 gallons from the end of our pipe lines and then pump it back into our tanks. That was to clean the pipe lines out, so that we could load our trucks and the peddler trucks, and any fishing boat or Coast Guard boat that would come to our dock for fuel. A barge usually meant over time and we were quick to volunteer for it. The first few truck loads drawing from these pipe lines were tested for water, and flash point tested, if gasoline, it was tested with a hydrometer, before it was allowed to be sold.

 Then around the first of March our supply of motor oil arrived by trailer truck. This would fill our motor oil warehouse up for the summer. Then around the middle of the month we would have our spring safety meeting, and that would be mixed in with a spring sales meeting, with a dinner in some nice hotel. I always looked forward to that as I would receive my safe driving pin. I drove 22 and a half years with out a motor vehicle accident. I want to say I didn't achieve this award alone, as Willard Sewall our station manager had a safety meeting once a month, and I received plenty of words of caution from fellow drivers.

 At this time Willard Sewall our station manager would post our vacation schedule. When I was on shift work this was always welcome, as then we would go on a 7 to 4 PM work schedule. For the first fifteen years I had Tuesdays as my day off. I always had the last pick on the vacation schedule, and had to take what was left. Some how during these times, I would some how worm a couple of weeks in June. One day I asked my boss, Willard Sewall, if I could do the days cash report? I was soon doing every days bookkeeping, then I started doing the end of the month bookkeeping, and the inventory. It wasn't long and Willard was using me on his days off. The other guy's didn't really like, what I was doing. Jim Wilcox was our Union president, and he worked in the Rockland plant, as a yard man. Jim came from the East Boston, Socony Vacuum Plant, and forced his way into the Rockland plant with his seniority rights. He was telling me that, when my time was up with the plant managers job. He wasn't going to let me back into the union. There was no love lost in our friendship. Then in the fall of 1961, Fred Bucklin our current plant manager, went on vacation and left me in charge of the plant. I was to be the plant manager for the month of October. At first I run the plant easily. Then Jim would start giving me a hard time. He was telling me, he wouldn't let me back into the union, when Fred Bucklin came back from his vacation. I also had a feeling, he was calling my district manager on his noon hour, and complaining about me. What was hard for me to except. For many years Charlie Maxcy another employee, had been acting plant manager. When the plant manager was on vacation, and he hadn't said a word to him. I was reluctant to call my district manager and talk to him about it. I was afraid he would think I couldn't handle my job, or my workman. That afternoon just before quitting time, I called my boss up and was going to talk to him about Jim. Instead I started to give him a hard time about being transferred. To this day I don't know where this rage came from. At this time, Vera was pregnant with Mary Jo, our third daughter. We had been up most of the night, when she was born after midnight, October 18 1961. Mary Jo was a beautiful little girl, and she took some of the sting out of my transfer to Bangor.

 When I went to work that next morning Mr. Gustafson came down from Portland, and told me, he was transferring me to Bangor, Maine the first of Dec. I hadn't been very happy with my job for a number of years, and I almost quit. I had just bought a nice 1958 Pontiac Safari station wagon. I owed around $2000.00 on it.

Also my sons were in high school, and I knew they would want to go to college. I had to swallow my pride and stay with the job. I moved to Bangor. It was hard to find a house to live in. I traveled to Bangor all winter.

Then in the spring I found Margie Kallock. She wanted to move back to Rockland; she had lost her husband in a hunting accident that fall. We swapped houses. I would load my station wagon with my household goods, haul them to Bangor, go to work, then after work, unload them at her house, then load her household goods in my car and go home. It was sixty-two miles one way to Bangor. I moved everything, even my piano, all in my car and a pick-up truck.

When I arrived in Bangor to start work, there sat the same old truck that I drove in Rockland. My job was to deliver fuel oil to the Air Force, Cape-Hart housing project. These were four houses in one building, with four fuel oil fill pipes. All in different places. That meant I had to haul that fuel oil hose four times for each house. There were around a hundred houses that I had to keep filled. I would go up one street, then down another. I resolved that, in time, I would quit Mobil Co.

The first thing I had to do was to get my high school diploma. I went to the University of Maine and took a battery of five tests, which would give me a high school equivalency diploma. I passed with a score of 3.50. Which was considered very good. Then I took a two-year course in Electrical Technology, with a major in electric motors. I passed with a score of 4.0. That was in 1964. As I was working back in Rockland, I didn't want to leave the company. The summer of 1967, the company decided to close down the Rockland plant, and once again I was transferred – this time to Portland, Maine.

I liked Portland, and thought I would stay there. When Jim Wilcox, our union president came down to Portland and put one of his friends in my job, and I had to go back to Bangor. As it happened, I bumped Howard Nelson. He went to Portsmouth, New Hampshire. This was also the second time I bumped him. I felt bad about it, so the next day after work, I went to see Howard. He was really mad at me. I explained what had taken place, and that I had nothing to do with the transfer. We left friends once again. The next day he died of a heart attack, at work. Now I knew I would quit. I left a job that paid $4.80 an hour, with five weeks paid vacation, unlimited medical care, a savings plan that matched my money dollar for dollar from the company, and an excellent retirement plan. The final straw came on the first day of January 1969. The union went out on strike, we were out for one month. I learned that I could make a living doing carpenter work, also, the company showed us who was boss, when it was time for our checks to come after working for two weeks without pay. Under "other" on our check stubs, they took what money was left and kept it. Then in March, we were to have a safety meeting. I would receive an award for 22 years of safe driving. The plant manager made up an accident report, that was supposed to have happened one night down in South West Harbor, Maine. When I returned to work the next day he tried to get me to sign the accident report. For the first time in my life, I told my boss he was a liar, and I would not sign his accident report. I went home and wrote my resignation. I gave it to him, two weeks before I was through.

It took a great deal of courage to do this. At forty-eight years of age, it wasn't easy. I had been trying to get a job with an electrical contractor for eight years, but nobody would hire me. I took a job with a fiberglass boat manufacturer at $2.25 an hour, and no benefits, six months in this new job, I was responsible for the general plant, store room, supplies, and the heating plant.

One day my friend Bob Philbrook asked me to install a hundred amp service for him. In the process I had to ask an electrical contractor to inspect it for me so I could get the Central Maine Power Co. to energize it for me. The contractor then asked me to go to work for him, which I did. I worked for him for about a year and a half, then I went to work for the Fisher Engineering Co. I made my Journeyman electrician license, and six months later I made my Masters Electrician license. I passed my Masters Electrician exam in September, just two years and nine months into the electrical trade. I went into my electrical contracting business January 1, 1973. I entered the most satisfying time of my life. It wasn't easy, and I found myself calling upon God and my faith much the same as I did years ago, when I was a young sailor in the far reaches of the Pacific Ocean on board the destroyer U.S.S. Hull DD 350.

I called my business "Mathieson Electric Inc." I had a sign painted on my truck (the first new vehicle I had ever owned). My logo was a big red ball with a white background, and the words Mathieson Electric Inc. painted around the outside edge of the red ball. Business was very good. At one time I had three new houses going at once, and all electric heat. I had taken an advanced bookkeeping course for two years at the high school when I worked for Mobil, Oil Corp. Now it came in handy. I set my business up in such a way that I could tell every night if I was making any money. I loved the work, and my company policy was to be HONEST. It was great fun and it passed very quickly.

Then in May 1965, the U.S.S. Mass. Reunion group managed to get control of the battleship. With the help of the Massachusetts school children and others, they raised around $135,000, and had the ship towed into Fall River, Massachusetts. I went down the spring of 1968 and went aboard. It was twenty-five years ago when I left her. I had forgotten how to go below. As I walked around the ship I met an old friend, Rob Case. He was the guy that met his girl in Boston and we would go out to Spectacle Island in Boston harbor. He was so tickled to see me again, we had to leave the ship and find a telephone, call home, and tell his kids that he had finally met his friend. Going aboard this great ship, it was like going to the morgue. It was dead. No motors. No sound. I felt very sad. Now, some thirty years later, it has come alive. Last spring I went aboard, and at the banquet at Whites Restaurant, I was honored with giving a short speech on my experience during the Casablanca battle. There were a couple of guys that were doing the firing of the guns, they came over right away and wanted me to tell them where these valves were in the ship, and how they worked. I went to many reunions and met a lot of old friends. On the fiftieth anniversary they fired the five inch guns for the first time since the war. What a thrill! Some of the guns didn't go off right away, as the powder was old. At first when I went to the reunions, I carried a feeling of remorse against my shipmates. I remembered the times back when I had so much trouble with my shipmates. But now that has disappeared, and we have much friendlier relationships and more respect than ever before.

Going aboard this great ship now, I have a sentimental feeling, because I realize what it has done for me. It brought me out here to the east coast, my wife Vera and the wonderful life she has brought me. Actually I credit the ship with bringing me to the coast of Maine.

In the spring of 1980, Mary came home from school and asked if she could have a sister. We thought she meant a real sister. Then she mentioned A.F.S. Well, we applied and that summer a very young girl from Australia arrived: Sandra Christie from Melbourne. She was just seventeen. When she arrived that evening, I tried to tell her not to fall in love, as she was just a little girl. But she didn't listen. She fell in love with a local boy, a lobster fisherman. Today they have a boy, Eon, and a girl, Alyssia. For her parents, Eric and Elaine Christie, that meant they would return to America every year for a month stay. Over the years, we have become fast friends. What was once a strained relationship is now full of understanding. Elaine said to me last summer, "Sandra is now an American. It is now October 1998, and I want to end this narrative of my life. I am soon to be 79 years old. There is much to be said of my life, its disappointments and accomplishments. I have been blessed with a rich family life.

Damage Profile showing 9 torpedoes

Bob Kinderman
Louis Mathieson

U.S.S. Arizona Model
12/7/1991 50th Reunion

My family
Left to right: Louis, Vera, Nancy Lou, Mary-Jo, John, Ann, James

Lobster Festival Parade
Alicia and Baby Jasimine, Erica, Vera, Matthew, Jason

*Left to right: Front row: (Bubber) Robert Jr., Ben, Bob Sr., Mary Lou
Back row: Denise, Louis, Janette D., Andy, Jim, Peggy Kindeman*

Reunion Aboard Ship
Rob Case, Vera, Helen, Louis

Waiting to receive our medals
Louis and Harry

Senator George Mitchell giving me my medal

Reunion time
Special time in Forward Emergency Diesel Generator Room

JEAN BART—Lies damaged at Casablanca. Her deck plates buckled and debris-laden, with a gaping hole torn in her side, the French battleship Jean Bart lies in Casablanca harbor, French West Africa. The ship was damaged by American Navy planes and shells in the African invasion.

Everett Mathieson SM 1/C, 1942

Company 37-40 USNTS Great Lakes, Illinois

Submitted by Harry Lapham (USS Tangier), 10744 I Dr. No., Battle Creek, MI 49014

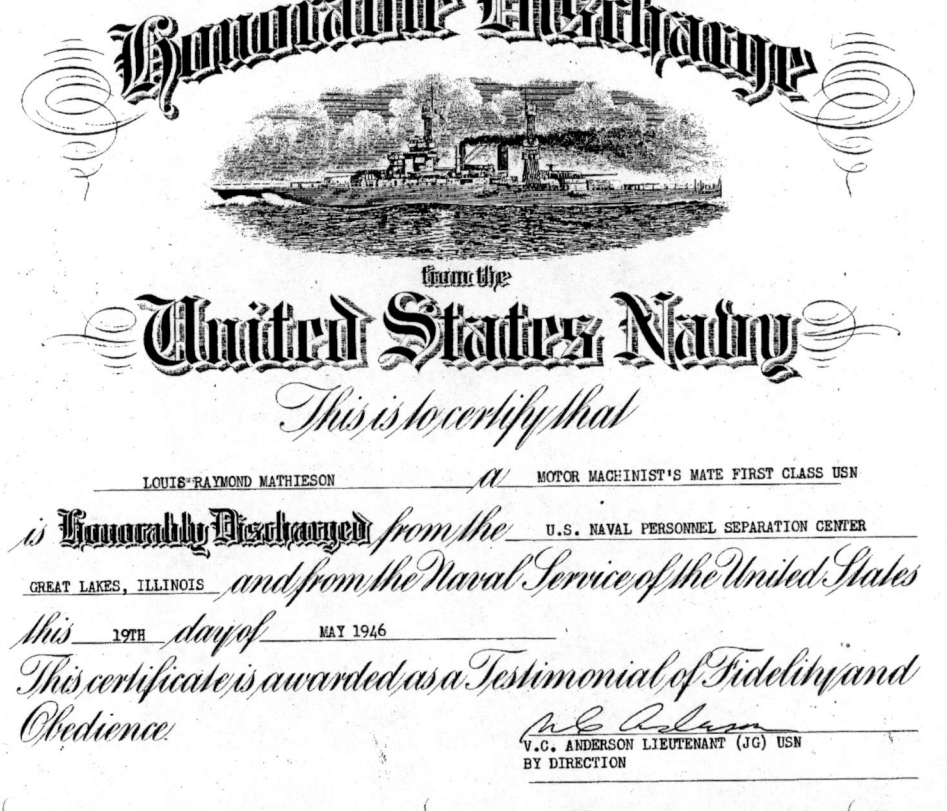

C2844733 Series C

Honorable Discharge

from the United States Navy

This is to certify that LOUIS RAYMOND MATHIESON a MOTOR MACHINIST'S MATE FIRST CLASS USN is Honorably Discharged from the U.S. NAVAL PERSONNEL SEPARATION CENTER GREAT LAKES, ILLINOIS, and from the Naval Service of the United States this 19TH day of MAY 1946

This certificate is awarded as a Testimonial of Fidelity and Obedience.

V.C. ANDERSON LIEUTENANT (JG) USN
BY DIRECTION

Lawrence and Jannet Pease
Louis and Vera Mathieson

Louis Mathieson

Fourth of July Parade 1995

Dear Louie,

I'm sorry this took so long but you know how it is with lawyers and estate settlements. It was very important to my dad that he left you something. I can tell you that you were his friend and shipmate for life and that was for always. Distance never mattered. During his last few months we often talked about your navy days together and while they were rough and terrible times they also forged a bond of friendship that cannot be stronger. I hope you find good use for the money and I'll keep in touch for sure. I'm late for work now and have to run. I'll write soon.

P.S. at Pa's funeral we played and sang "Anchors Aweigh" as he left the church. It really fit.

Bob Kinderman
Standing by the throttle in Number One Engine Room.
We have four engine rooms.

Pearl Harbor Survivors Association

SIXTH DISTRICT
Alabama, Florida, Mississippi, S. Carolina,
Georgia, Kentucky, Tennessee, N. Carolina

PAST DIRECTOR DISTRICT 6
Samuel D. Smith
P.O. Box 941
Elon College, NC 27244
(919) 584-0771

March 4 - 83

Dear Lou :

Certainly I'm not one to ordinarily believe in ghosts but yesterday, more than at anytime before - seeing you again makes me convinced I had better give it some thought and re-evaluation - maybe I do ?

Enclosed you will find not only the roster list of those of us did survive the Okie and also the letter from the Keninger family we spoke of (you were correct about Kinderman) in my own defense however, Keninger was on watch with me in the forward dynamo plant and that being his battle station I never seen him again after Charlie Swanson relieved me to go to repair 5. I'm sure you will find the roster list answering some of your questions - hope so.

Sending along a few bits and pieces you might find to your liking as well with this admonition - do wish you would attend the New Orleans Okie reunion so give it some thought.

Looking forward to hearing from you so drop a line when convenient.

Best possible regards,

Sam

Samuel D.

Don't recall exact date, but I do know it was during the Hunters Point drydocking in San Francisco when we replaced the fractured shaft.

Pearl Harbor Survivors Association

SIXTH DISTRICT
Alabama, Florida, Mississippi, S. Carolina,
Georgia, Kentucky, Tennessee, N. Carolina

PAST DIRECTOR DISTRICT 6
Samuel D. Smith
P.O. Box 941
Elon College, NC 27244
(919) 584-0771

April 8 - 83

Dear Lou :

No question about it - We have finally made the 'big time'.
We've gotta be candidates for the 'Thats Incredible' show .

Received your letter and accompanying material yesterday and
continually thinking of it since. The paralleling accounts are
almost unreal, incredible, if you will ?

To proove the point - the accounting of staff writer David Jeffers
"Pearl Harbor Story Retold At Lily Bay" and carried in the Camden
Herald on August 4 - 77 and the untitled personal chronology of
March 1960 and now, my own chronology of recent vintage - most any-
one could make a pretty good 'court case' all the articles were
written by the same person - they are that similar.

From my point of view a thought provoking puzzle keeps cropping up.
To my recollection, neither of us these many years had communicated
in any way, shape or form and I personally have no knowledge of any
meeting whatsoever. Why then I ask myself, prompted you to detour
from your likely route home to seek me out. I in no way consider myself mystical in any sense of the word nor you in fact of the matter
but you just cant discount there had to be some reason, 'spooky' as
it seems to be. Think about it ? Some magnetism between us must exist
and we never knew it till now ?

If you could locate the staff writer David Jeffers and lay before him
these three letters of evidence I would be curious what his comments
would be ! True - we both were at the sameplace, same time and same
event and our accounts are factual to support our writings but why
after all this elapsed time does it surface but more to the point,
out of somewhere in outer space you in fact 'knock on my door'.

To avoid any misunderstanding I have made copies of the newspaper
article and your typewritten chronology and returning them to your
safekeeping. In doing so however, I think you will beleive me when
I tell you in some curious, undecipherable way, its like mailing
myself ?

Sorry you and Harry and Kinderman cant make the New Orleans reunion
but do mark your calendar for the same time period for next year as
we will be returning to Dubuque, Iowa where we unveiled the Father
Schmitt Memorial Plague and opened the park in his honor.

Running out of space - your material will follow during the week :

Sam
Samuel D.

Remember Pearl Harbor — Keep America Alert!

Pearl Harbor Survivors Association

SIXTH DISTRICT
Alabama, Florida, Mississippi, S. Carolina,
Georgia, Kentucky, Tennessee, N. Carolina

PAST DIRECTOR DISTRICT 6
Samuel D. Smith
P.O. Box 941
Elon College, NC 27244
(919) 584-0771

April 15 - 83

Dear Lou / Vera :

Thought it desirable to get in a word or two before sealing the enclosed material of yours. I do want to go on record that any time the notion prompts you dont hesitate to drop me a line or two and rest assured, I will do the same.

Keep in mind the USS Oklahoma reunion in Dubuque, Iowa next time and try to make it. It is always the last week in May to coincide with her commissioning date. The Navy League of Dubuque can be depended on to put on an outstanding affair in our behalf.

Well its almost shift change so I will seal this and get on with the 'plan of the day'

Say hellotoall and takecareofyourself.

Sam
Samuel D.

Remember Pearl Harbor — Keep America Alert!

State of Maine

129967

ELECTRICIANS EXAMINING BOARD

Be it known that   LOUIS R MATHIESON

Has qualified as required by MRSA, Title   032   Chapter   000017

IS AUTHORIZED TO ACT AS A/AN
MASTER ELECTRICIAN

AUTHORIZED SIGNATURE

Susan M. Collins

LIC/CERT/REG #   MST00102929   ISSUE DATE   10-19-88   EXPIRES   10-31-90   ORIGINAL LIC DATE   9-19-72

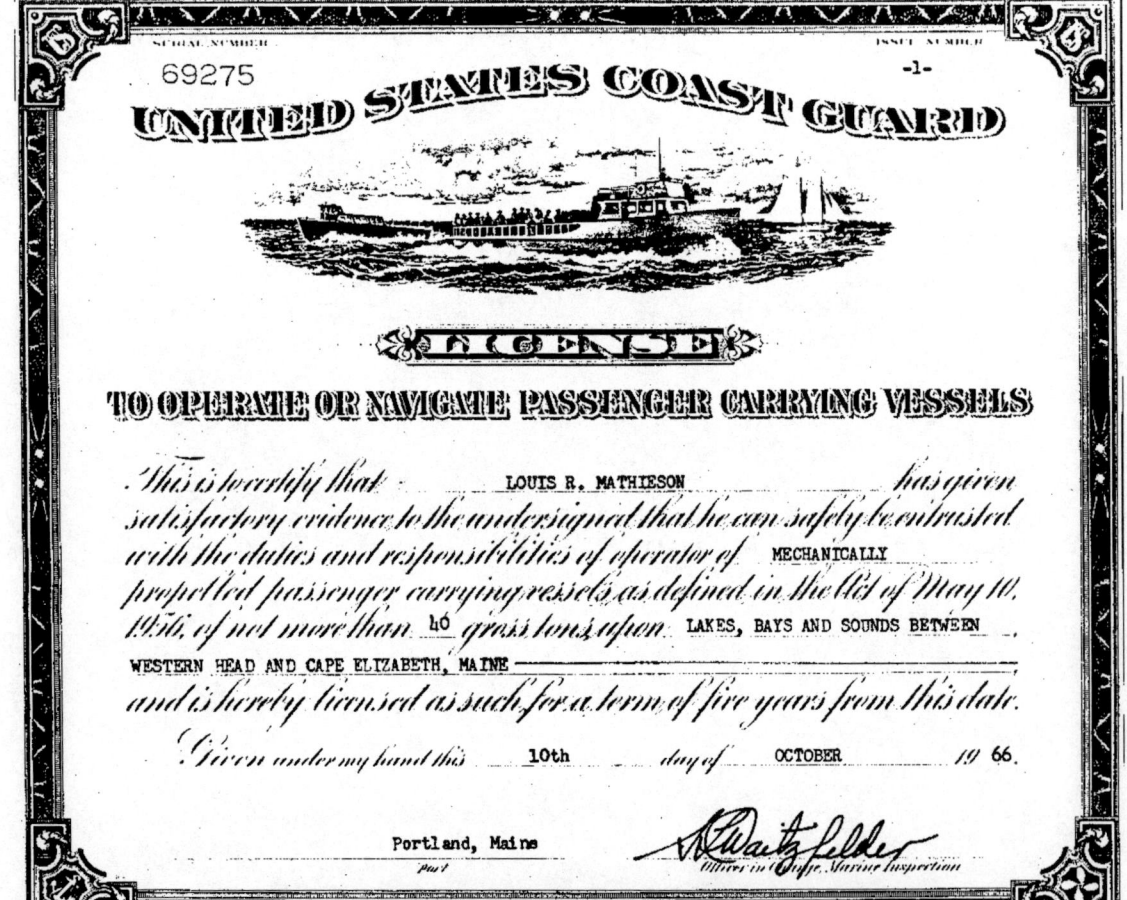

SERIAL NUMBER 69275   ISSUE NUMBER -1-

UNITED STATES COAST GUARD

LICENSE
TO OPERATE OR NAVIGATE PASSENGER CARRYING VESSELS

This is to certify that LOUIS R. MATHIESON has given satisfactory evidence to the undersigned that he can safely be entrusted with the duties and responsibilities of operator of MECHANICALLY propelled passenger carrying vessels as defined in the Act of May 10, 1956, of not more than 40 gross tons upon LAKES, BAYS AND SOUNDS BETWEEN WESTERN HEAD AND CAPE ELIZABETH, MAINE and is hereby licensed as such for a term of five years from this date.

Given under my hand this 10th day of OCTOBER 19 66.

Portland, Maine
Port

Officer in Charge, Marine Inspection

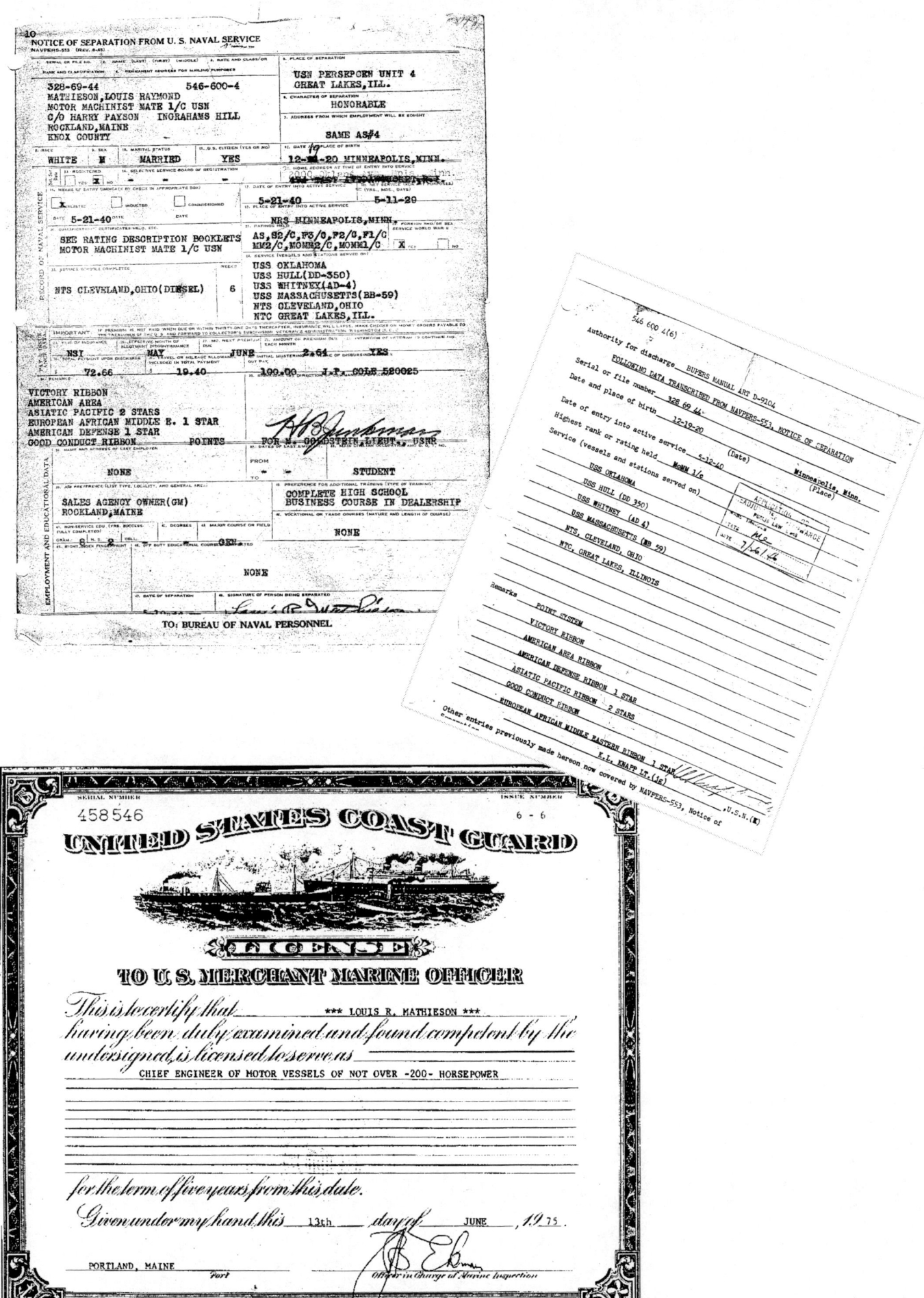

Harry & Louis Mathieson
Summer 1991

Alan Mathieson
Jason Johnson
Louis Mathieson
Matthew Jeffers
*My grandsons onboard
USS Massachusetts BB59*

Louis Mathieson
Andy Mathieson
Vera Mathieson
*December 7, 1991 – Pearl Harbor
Arizona Memorial is across the bay.*

Andy was on the USS Ingersol DD.

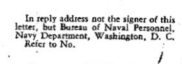

```
                    NAVY DEPARTMENT
                    BUREAU OF NAVAL PERSONNEL
                    WASHINGTON 25, D. C.

Pers-   824C-dhm
        328 69 44

28 November 1947


Mr. Louis Raymond Mathieson
Ingraham's Hill
Rockland, Maine

Dear Mr. Mathieson:

    The following transcript of your naval service
is forwarded as requested in your letter of
recent date:

22 May 40   Enl in USN as Apprentice Seaman at
            Minneapolis, Minnesota.
22 May 40   T to NTS, Great Lakes, Illinois.
13 Aug 40   T to USS OKLAHOMA
30 Sep 40   CR to Seaman second class.
10 Oct 40   CR to Fireman third class.
16 Feb 41   CR to Fireman second class.
 1 Jul 41   CR to Fireman first class.
 9 Dec 41   T to USS HULL
18 Jan 42   R on board USS SOLACE
 9 Feb 42   T to USS WHITNEY
25 Feb 42   T to R/S Pearl Harbor, T.H., FFT
 4 May 42   R at R/S New York, N.Y.
 8 May 42   T to RS, Boston, Mass.
12 May 42   T to USS MASSACHUSETTS
 1 Oct 42   CR to Machinist's Mate second class.
23 Dec 43   T to Nearest R/S, W.C., U.S., FFT
19 Jan 44   R at RecShip, San Francisco, California.
18 Mar 44   T to NTSch(Diesel), Cleveland, Ohio
12 Apr 44   CR to Motor Machinist's Mate second class.
 3 Aug 44   T to USNH, Great Lakes, Illinois.
14 Aug 44   T to NTSch(Diesel) Cleveland, Ohio.
 2 Nov 44   CR to Motor Machinist's Mate first class.
 5 Feb 46   T to Service Schools Command, NTC, Great Lakes, Ill.
15 Apr 46   T to USNH, Great Lakes, Ill.
25 Apr 46   T to Service Schools Command, NTC, Great Lakes, Ill.
16 May 46   T to PSC, Great Lakes, Ill.
19 May 46   Dis from PSC, Great Lakes, Ill., as Motor Machinist's Mate fir
            class, with an Honorable Discharge.
            No time lost.

Date and place of birth: 19 December 1920, Minneapolis, Minn.

By direction of Chief of Naval Personnel:
                                    Sincerely yours,

                                    A. R. ROMANOWSKI
                                    CHSCLK, USN, Records Activity.
```

My grandsons
Matthew D Jeffers, Jason Johnson, and Grandpa

Jason, Catie Rose, Erica
6 years, 4 years, 7 years

Ian Curtis and Lucas Smalley
Summer 1992

Senator Margurite Chase Smith
Neil Hill
Skowhegan, Maine 04976
Dec. 19 1993

Senator Margurite Chase Smith

I am writing to you in regard to the loose leaf note book given to you by Mr.& Mrs. Richard Spear. This was the story of my life, by Louis R. Mathieson. I would like you to keep this story as long as nobody uses it for commercial purposes, or uses it for any other purpose, without my personal permission. I wrote this for my children, so that they could pass it on to their children. I consider it an honor for you to accept this story, to be kept in your library.

Do you remember our conversation about this book, when I was visiting last fall with Mr. & Mrs. Spear. You suggested that I engage a journalist to write this book for me and have it printed. I have not found a journalist or a writer to do this. I am still looking for some body. I have another retired person that I intend to try. If I can

I wanted you to have this story as I think it will be useful some day for some other young person who might be studying the history of world war II. I feel that my story would be safe in your library.

Louis R. Mathieson

P.S. Perhaps you will keep this letter with my story?

Margaret Chase Smith

December 22, 1993

Dear Louis Mathieson:

Thank you for your thoughtful note which will be placed with the material you write me about. I am pleased if you feel your story will be well kept here and am sure researchers will find much use in your written words.

With best wishes for happy holidays.

Sincerely,

Neil Hill - Skowhegan, Maine 04976

November 7, 1993
Senator Margurite Chase Smith
Skowkegan, Maine

Top: Camden, Maine 1964 – Louis ?? I can't get up over the hill in Camden as it is too icy. I drove 22 1/2 years for Mobil Oil without a motor vehicle accident.

Center: May 1968, onboard USS Massachusetts – first time since December 1943. Robert and Hellen Case, Vera and Louis Mathieson. Our first reunion in 21 years. Rob was one of my men, we went ashore together. I was his best man on their wedding day.

*Bottom Left: John's graduation from the Maine Maritime Academy.
Nancy, Vera, James, Ann, John, Me, Mary Jo*

Bottom Right: John Mathieson and Dad Louis R. Mathieson standing in front of the Maine Yankee Nuclear Power Plant, June 1995.

*Harry Mathieson, and Elena Fredette
(Owl's Head Town Clerk)*

*Irving Curtis American Legion
Harry, Louis, Eleanor Fredette, L.W.
Gustafson, Division Operating Manager
Socony Vaccuum Oil Co. Inc.*

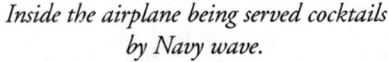

*Bob and Marine Colonel, Secretary of the
Navy's Airplane, 1960.*

*Inside the airplane being served cocktails
by Navy wave.*

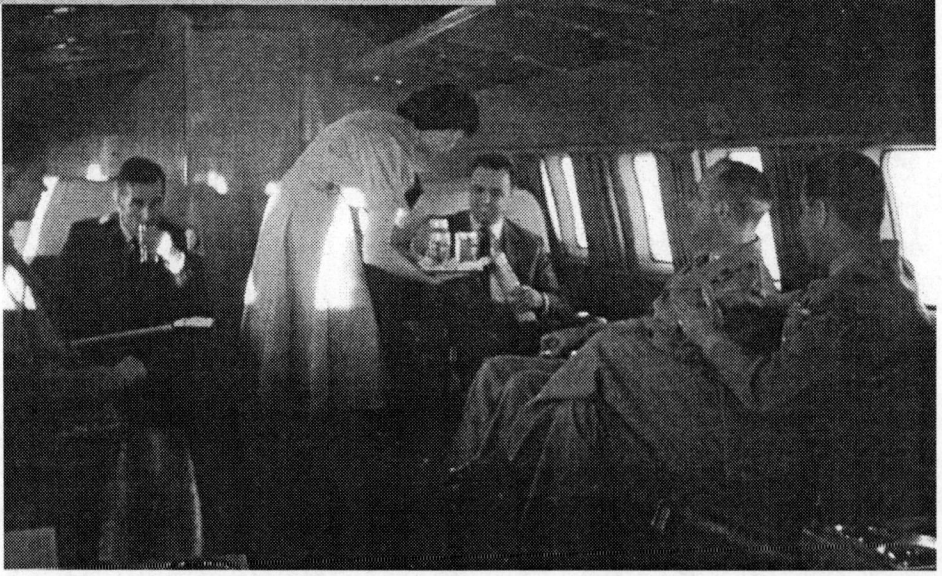

Admiral King and Admiral Arleigh Burke during the dedication of U.S.S. Oklahoma anchor

Louis Mathieson, the school teacher I met

Louis Mathieson, George Adams, Harry Mathieson, and Bob Kinderman

Left to right: Louis Mathieson, George DeLong, Vivian MsCouc?, Robert Kinderman, Harry Mathieson

Bob Kinderman, Harry Mathieson

Admiral King, Admiral Arleigh Burke (31 Knot Burke) at the dedication of the U.S.S. Oklahoma anchor.

Rockland Congregational Church
Sunday December 7, 1997
Betsey Audet, Pastor

Children's Sermon, delivered by Louie Mathieson

Good morning!

I have in my hand some coins—pennies (pass out to each child a penny). On each there is a slogan; can you read it? Is it, in GOD WE TRUST? This same slogan is on every coin the U. S. government makes. My story today is how I trusted GOD a long time ago.

It was just 56 years ago on this date Dec. 7, 1941. It was a Sunday morning in a place called Pearl Harbor, Hawaii. The day was not much different than today. We were getting ready for church services on deck. I had the 4 to 8 A.M. watch in the refrigeration plant on board the Battleship USS Oklahoma. Here is a picture of it. I was relieved 15 minutes early, so as to take a shower. I removed all of my clothes at my watch station and with a towel around my middle, I went up three decks to the main deck and across the ship to the engineer's washroom. As I stepped into the shower stall, our general alarm sounded and we were required to go immediately to our battle stations. My station was repair 5 in the machine shop. I was totally naked except for my shoes.

We received our first of nine torpedo hits. The deck under me came up about a foot and a half, throwing me into the air, and as I came down the second hit came and the deck came up to meet me. I was thrown about much like a candlepin in a bowling alley. The lights went out, and I was very frightened. I thought I should say a prayer. I tried the Lord's Prayer, 'OUR FATHER WHO ART IN HEAVEN', when we were hit again by two more torpedoes. My thoughts were scattered, so this time I tried the Twenty-Third Psalm, "THE LORD IS MY SHEPHERD I SHALL NOT WANT. HE LEADETH… we were hit by two more torpedoes. Then I thought: I don't have time to say a prayer. I then said "LORD, I PLACE MY LIFE IN YOUR HANDS". Now all of a sudden I could think, my fear was gone. Shortly after this the word was to abandon ship.

When we tried to open ways to escape, we learned that we were underwater; we were trapped. I said to my friend next to me, "What about that opening up there in the ceiling? Do you suppose it will lead us out of here? Get on my shoulders and I'll help up there." He said, "No, you go." So I went up. It was a very narrow shaft, just big enough for me to stretch my arms over my head and wiggle my way up, using my toes and my fingers. Now my thoughts were, would I meet up with an obstruction in this shaft, and would the hatch cover on deck be open? The cover was closed and locked tight in battle. I knew that. Now I had to "TRUST GOD" to see that this hatch would be open for me. I remember that part of the BIBLE where JESUS walked upon the water in the Sea of Galilee and Paul was walking on the water, too, until he looked back at his friends on the boat, than he sank into the water. My temptation was to turn back, as I realized that I couldn't open that hatch from the inside. But I didn't, I kept on going as I looked up into the eyes of GOD I could make it.

I reached the top and the hatch was open. I crawled out and turned and called down to my shipmates, "Come on up, guys, the hatch is open." I stood there bare naked, with all of the bombs falling, and bullets flying around and a fire nearby. I helped my friends out as quickly as possible. When the last one was out, the ship rolled over on top of us. The next thing I knew, I was out in the harbor swimming in that black heavy fuel oil and water.

Many years later, my brother Harry, told me that he met the sailor that opened that hatch, that morning. He said that he was going by there, when a thought came to him that somebody might want to escape through there. What is interesting, this sailor had fourteen years service, and was a first class petty officer, and he knew the penalty could result in a general court martial and death by a firing squad.

I learned one important lesson that day: To put my TRUST IN GOD.

Will you help me sing this song? Jesus loves me, yes I know, For the Bible tells me so, little ones to him belong, We are weak but he is strong, Yes Jesus loves me, Yes Jesus loves me, Yes Jesus loves me for the Bible tells me so.

Now maybe we can say a prayer—a prayer that I used all those bad days during the war.

Now I lay me down to sleep, I pray the lord my soul to keep, if I should die before I wake, I pray the LORD my soul to keep.

Quick Order Form

Fax orders: 603.806.5832
Phone orders: 207.594.8149
Email orders: support@bullioncoin.com
Postal orders: MCS, Ltd, Mark Smalley, PO Box 972, Camden ME 04843 USA

Please send _____ copies of *One Sunday Morning* by Louis Mathieson,
ISBN# 0-9717008-0-xX, at **$19.95** per copy
I understand that I may return the books for a full refund—for any reason, no questions asked.

Name _____

Address _____

City _____ State _____ PostalCode _____

Country _____

Telephone_____ Email _____

Sales Tax: Please add 5.5% for books shipped to Maine addresses.

Shipping options:
USPS Priority: First book $5.00 ($3.50 for each additional)
USPS Book rate: First book $3.00 ($2.50 each additional)
International: $12.50 first book ($10.00 for each additional - estimate)

Bulk wholesale orders: Please call, email or fax request.

We only accept money orders, cashiers checks and personal/business checks at this time.

Thank you!